IT **HAS** HAPPENED HERE

IT HAS

HAPPENED HERE

BY VIRGIL T. BLOSSOM

Let every man remember that to violate
the law is to trample on the blood of
his father, and to tear that charter of
his own and his children's liberty.
—Abraham Lincoln

HARPER & BROTHERS, NEW YORK

To my wife, Clarrene,
and our daughters, Bette Sue and Gail,
for their uncomplaining
devotion through it all.

*I wish to express my deep appreciation
for the able assistance of
Mr. Joe Alex Morris
in the preparation of this book.*

Contents

Contents

Foreword

THIS BOOK CONCERNS an effort to bring about a major change in the cultural pattern of an American city and the controversy it aroused. When emotions run strong there are likely to be misunderstandings and there is one point I would like to make clear at the beginning in regard to the use in this book of the term "segregationist." The large majority of the residents of Little Rock were opposed in principle to integration of Negro and white public schools and therefore they were segregationists. At the same time, this majority believed in obedience to the law of the land, and they should never be regarded as part of the movement of extreme segregationists whose defiance of the federal government brought on the Little Rock school crisis. In this book, for the most part, my use of the word "segregationists" refers to the active, organized extremist minority and should not be taken to mean the sincere and law-abiding citizens opposed to the principle of integration.

I would like to express my appreciation to members of the various Boards of Education who steadfastly followed the precepts of democratic procedure throughout the crisis, often when they were personally opposed in principle to the ultimate goal. The vote at Board meetings almost always was six to none or five to one, with Dr. Dale Alford dissenting in behalf of the segregationists.

The Central Administrative staff and the school staff generally demonstrated their devotion to good citizenship and to the children, despite the fact that they might not personally agree with the school integration decisions of the Supreme Court. I cannot say too much in regard to their loyalty and their hard work under trying conditions. I was also proud of the poise and decency of the vast majority of students in a period of great emotional strain. And I wish to thank the many members of the Parent-Teacher Association, the School Board's legal staff and countless community leaders who gave their best efforts to an intelligent approach to a grave national problem.

Their defeat—if it was a defeat—can be only temporary.

V. T. B.

New York
1959

IT **HAS** HAPPENED HERE

Chapter One

TRAGEDY HITS A
BOOMING CITY

HOW DO YOU CHANGE the character of a city of 120,000 souls in only a year? You can tear down a city in perhaps a few months as Carthage was leveled by the Romans. You can bomb it into rubble in a few hours as the heart of Rotterdam was bombed. You can atomize it in a few seconds as Hiroshima was atomized.

But can you, by force or fear, change the social and political complexion of a modern American city in a matter of twelve or eighteen months? My unhappy answer is that you can if you are willing to resort to the weapons of bigotry and intimidation and demagoguery and the awful presence of mobs in the street.

In the spring of 1957, the city of Little Rock, Arkansas, seemed to me to be one of the most pleasant and progressive communities in America. It was a friendly, open-handed town where the easy comradeship of the West and the hustling spirit of the Middle West blended with the traditions of the Old South. It was the state capital but it was also a booming, vigorous business center, spreading out rapidly along the broad, snakelike curves of the torpid Arkansas River. It served a quarter of a million persons in the immediate area, its population was steadily increasing and the average spending of its families was more than $5,000 a year. No less than thirty-four new industrial plants had been attracted to the community within a few years and others were planning to move into a new six-hundred-acre industrial district.

But, more important than rising bank deposits and rising value of manufactured products shown on the Chamber of Commerce charts, the people of Little Rock were proud of and ambitious for their community. They planned ahead and they kept abreast of the mainstream of progress. They had fourteen hospitals and a dozen nursing homes. They had six parks that covered fifteen hundred acres. They had two junior colleges, one graduate center, one liberal arts college and the university medical school. They had a $4,000,000 public school building program—including two new high schools that were near completion—to provide the most modern facilities for some twenty thousand pupils. Although the state was usually ranked near the bottom of the list in education, the city's high schools were fully accredited by the North Central Association of Colleges and Secondary Schools and Central High School was regarded as among the best in the nation.

Little Rock was proud, too, of its reputation as a city of excellent race relations. Buses, hospitals and certain other public facilities were integrated. Biracial meetings commonly strove in a spirit of harmony to solve community problems. Negro and white employees worked side by side on many jobs with a minimum of tension or friction. And, despite a general, traditional attitude in favor of segregation, the majority of residents were prepared—reluctantly—to accept the United States Supreme Court 1954 school desegregation decision as the law of the land and to initiate a program of gradual integration of Negro students into Central High School.

That was in the spring of 1957.

In 1958, Little Rock was a different city. I don't mean that it looked different. The tall office buildings, the bulbous dome of the state capitol, the hospitals, the new schools, the parks and the factories were still there. But the character of the city was not at all the same. A ruthless, whirlwind campaign of bigotry, of political pressure, of economic boycott and of mob violence—initiated mainly from outside the city—had drastically transformed the social and economic condition of the community. An extremist minority had seized control. The public senior high schools were closed by proclamation of the Governor to thwart integration. The public school system was demoralized. The sparkle was rubbed off the business boom and for almost two years, up to the day this is written, not a single new industry had decided to move into the Little Rock industrial area.

But these were only the most obvious signs of damage which will require years of arduous effort to repair. By the end of 1958, relations between the races were bitter and antagonistic. Co-operation or even normal communication between the white and Negro communities had deteriorated or virtually ceased. The white community was divided and confused. Many school children were taught to parrot the scurrilous phrases of segregationist propaganda. Men who advocated moderation were the targets of vicious economic boycott, and the threat of boycott silenced many civic leaders whose services were desperately needed. State legislators, with hardly a dissenting vote, handed over unprecedented powers to the Governor. Free speech was almost negated by a reign of fear.

"You had all just as well recognize," a leading businessman told a private conference of the city's most prominent men in 1958, "that we are living in a police state."

The change that occurred in Little Rock was undeserved and humiliating to the helpless majority of residents. It was a heavy blow to everyone and particularly to me as Superintendent of Schools. But, regardless of the future course of events, it is probable that what happened at Little Rock will remain a unique case history to be studied by experts in the future just as army officers from all over the world once studied the Battle of Gettysburg as a rare and enlightening example of military tactics.

All of the elements—decency and demagoguery, intensity and indifference—involved in the nation's grave school integration crisis were present at Little Rock. It is unlikely that ever again in this struggle over civil rights will there be a more clear-cut issue of respect for and obedience to the law, or that organized propaganda, economic pressures and selfish political scheming will again be so artfully combined to turn the optimum situation into a national disaster.

Little Rock did not bring on disaster. Disaster was deliberately thrust upon a majority of progressive and law-abiding citizens by extremists and outsiders seeking to serve their own ends. That is the story I now want to tell as frankly and as honestly as possible in the hope that it may be of some assistance to many fine men and women searching for an honorable solution to the integration crisis that will preserve our system of free public education in the South.

II

What happened to me at Little Rock is unimportant, but it is only fair that I explain something of my background as a school administrator and educator and that I make clear my own attitude toward the 1954 and 1955 decisions of the United States Supreme Court requiring school desegregation "with all deliberate speed."

My own feeling was that the Court's decision should have been delayed until a later date. But, once the decision was handed down, I firmly believed in respect for and honest compliance with the law of the land.

The first thirty years of my career in the field of education were spent in Arkansas and Oklahoma. But I was born in Brookfield, Missouri, where my father was city collector for twenty-nine years.

As a boy, I was big and strong enough to be tackle on the high school football team and catcher on the baseball team. I also got into some mischief—I can't remember what—in my junior year and was punished by the principal, who gave me the choice of staying after school for a month or entering the school oratory contest. I chose the contest and quickly discovered that scholastic achievement could be as exciting as football. I won a score of gold medals in contests with other schools in the next two years and was defeated only once.

When I finished high school there wasn't enough money for college, but I worked at various jobs in the town and also became a clerk in the Legislature at Jefferson City, graduating at the age of eighteen to be reading clerk in the Senate. In 1926, I got an athletic scholarship—the kind I had to work at—to attend Missouri Valley College at Marshall. I majored in education and got my degree in 1930. Later I received my master of science degree from the University of Arkansas and also took special courses at Northwestern University in Chicago.

I got out of Missouri Valley College in the worst days of the big Depression and was lucky to get a job teaching and coaching athletics in the high school at Fayetteville, Arkansas. The schools were understaffed, the work was hard and my pay of $150 a month was cut 33⅓ per cent in the next year. I decided to quit but changed my mind at the last moment when I met Miss Clarrene Tribble, daughter of the Mayor of Fayetteville, and fell in love. We were married in 1934 and have two daughters.

In 1935, I went to Okmulgee, Oklahoma, as teacher and athletic director but three years later returned to Fayetteville as principal of the high school on the understanding I would later become superintendent of schools, which I did in 1942. One of my first acts as superintendent was to expand facilities for education of Negro children. The public attitude toward school integration varies a great deal from state to state, usually depending on the percentage of Negro population. It also varies within Arkansas to a marked degree. In eastern Arkansas, a rich, flat farming area along the Mississippi River known as the Delta Country, there has always been strong opposition to any relaxation of segregation. As you move west through the state, this attitude changes. The attitude of Little Rock, in the center of the state, was less intolerant while that of Fayetteville, in the northwest, was still more progressive and under the influence of liberal-minded personnel at the University of Arkansas.

There were comparatively few Negro students in Fayetteville and they had never had a senior high school. I worked out, with the co-operation of the Board of Education, a system that enabled eligible Negro children to attend senior high school at a Negro school in Fort Smith, sixty-five miles away, with the Fayetteville school district paying transportation, living and school expenses. The state law prohibited them from attending white schools.

It was while I was superintendent at Fayetteville that the University of Arkansas accepted the first Negro, Silas Hunt, into its graduate law school without creating any public reaction. There have been a dozen or more Negroes in the graduate schools—and larger numbers in summer sessions—ever since. There has never been any public protest against integration of the graduate school, which was handled with good judgment and strictly as an administrative matter by former President Louis Webster Jones and President of the Board of Trustees Herbert L. Thomas.

In the eleven years I was at Fayetteville as Superintendent of Schools, the city grew rapidly and the school system was greatly expanded and reorganized. We annexed seventeen adjacent school districts that had had no high school facilities. Community leaders looked ahead to future educational problems. They formed a remarkable volunteer community group that promoted increases in school revenue, almost doubled the school budget, spent close to $2,000,000 for a new high school and elementary school improvements and helped raise another $200,000 for a handsome athletic field and community recreation area.

Fayetteville became a kind of showplace that was studied by many educators from other parts of the country as an example of what could be done to improve the school program and school facilities "in the backwoods." In 1953, city officials, civic clubs and the churches organized what they called "Virgil Blossom Appreciation Day" and presented me with a distinguished citizen award. Actually, this was a farewell gesture to me because in January of 1953 I had signed a contract to become Superintendent of Schools at Little Rock. I was not supposed to start the new job until July 1, but due to a series of complications the Little Rock post became vacant in February and for the next five months I served as Superintendent of Schools in both cities, more or less commuting between them.

The Little Rock School Board was in the midst of a big expansion program. A proposal for an eight-mill increase in the tax levy was to be submitted to the voters in March as part of a program for $4,000,000 in new school construction, and my first big task was to promote a favorable vote on the increase. Fortunately, it was approved by a two-to-one margin and construction was soon started. I might say here that I believe I have built more public buildings in Arkansas than anyone in the state's history, including three major high schools, two junior high schools, six elementary schools and additions—some very large—to sixteen other schools.

Late in the spring of 1953 I had to make a trip to New York to consult with Wall Street financial experts on handling the $4,000,000 bond issue. At one office I visited I happened to be glancing through a magazine when my attention was caught by a drawing that showed a young Negro looking at the glistening white marble home of the Supreme Court in Washington. The Court at that time had under consideration the so-called five "great cases" on integration of schools, technically known under the title of the first case—*Brown v. The Board of Education* at Topeka, Kansas. All five cases had been before the Court since 1952 and had been argued and reargued but were still undecided. They presented a variety of related situations but it was obvious that they represented a major legal effort to force desegregation of public schools in the South.

Looking at the drawing, I was struck by the questioning look in the eyes of the Negro and by the caption: "Will the Court have the courage?"

That picture and that question popped back into my mind many times as I went about my business in New York and returned to Little Rock. I kept thinking that this might well be my problem one of these days, just as it was now the problem of nine men sitting in Washington. Finally, I brought the subject up at a meeting of the School Board. I told them about the picture.

"Perhaps," I went on, "we ought to begin now to study in a preliminary way what we would have to do if the Court orders an end to segregation in the schools. It might be wise to have some kind of plan."

There wasn't much comment or much enthusiasm in response to my remarks, but in the end the president of the Board summed it up by saying: "Let's wait until we come to that bridge before we try to cross it."

I nodded my agreement. But then I didn't realize how close we were to the bridge. None of us did.

Chapter Two

THE BOARD OF
EDUCATION PREPARES
FOR COMPLIANCE

ON THE MORNING of May 17, 1954, I was very much aware that
the Supreme Court of the United States was in session in Washington and that it might act on the case of *Brown v. The Board of
Education*—actually meaning the five cases that would decide the
legality of racial segregation in public schools in our nation.

The cases had originally been brought in Kansas, South Carolina, Virginia, Delaware and the District of Columbia and, of
course, each case was listed on the Supreme Court docket under a
different name. But *Brown v. The Board of Education* at Topeka,
Kansas, was first on the alphabetical listing and everybody knew
that the Court's action in the Brown case would be decisive. I
had done a great deal of thinking about what that decision might
mean to our school system and I suppose I was a bit on edge when
the telephone on my desk rang. It was one of the reporters on a
Little Rock newspaper.

"The Supreme Court has just ruled on the Brown case," he said. "In effect, the decision says that states cannot enforce racial segregation in public schools. In other words, our segregated system is illegal regardless of whether equal school facilities are provided for white and colored children. The decision was unanimous. Would you give me some comment on the decision and what the Little Rock schools are going to do about it?"

I pointed out to him that as Superintendent of Schools I was not in a position to say what the School Board would do, but I said I doubted that the Supreme Court would try to force Southern or border states to take any hasty action in such an important matter. We would, I said, have to do a great deal of work in order to know the best course to follow.

The reporter hung up but my telephone kept on ringing. There were other newspapermen with questions and I also talked to members of the Board of Education, which was headed by Dr. William G. Cooper, Jr., a surgeon who was born in New York and who, I knew, was in no manner unrealistic as to the problems raised by the Court's decision.

The six-member School Board met the next day to discuss procedure. I would like to make it very clear that the people of Little Rock generally were opposed to the principle of the Supreme Court decision on school integration. They wanted to avoid integration if that were legally possible and, if not, they wanted a legal minimum of integration. There were also in the community a minority of segregation extremists who favored defiance of the Supreme Court decision, regardless of the consequences, but they were a distinct minority in a law-abiding city.

The School Board's official position was opposed to the principle of school integration as decreed by the Court but at our first meeting to consider future steps it was significant that not a single member expressed any idea of refusing to obey the law of the land. In fact, the meeting decided that the Board should soon issue a statement of policy and that I should take charge of preliminary planning of how and when we would comply with the Court's decision. Any definite steps, however, would have to await more definite instructions from the Court.

I consulted with many persons in the next few days. With the approval of the Board, I asked three prominent Negro leaders to arrange a meeting of a representative group to discuss our plans so they would know the Board's position before any public statement was made. The meeting began with much enthusiasm on the part of the Negroes because of the Court decision. I said that the Board would issue a statement the next day, May 22, as follows:

STATEMENT OF LITTLE ROCK BOARD OF EDUCATION
SUPREME COURT DECISION—SEGREGATION IN PUBLIC SCHOOLS

The Board of Education of Little Rock School District has been working for a number of years at the job of providing a program of separate but equal educational opportunities for all children of this city. During this period the problems of school finance, facilities, personnel, instructional supplies and other lesser items in our budgets have called for increased financial support. The accelerated birth rate and the growth of Little Rock have already overloaded our schools. Growth in school population will continue. This continued growth will require additional finances. The citizens of Little Rock have always responded to school needs in a splendid manner. The response of our citizens has made it possible to have and maintain our school program in its present form. To date this program has been in harmony with the Federal Constitutional requirements, and the statutory requirements of the State of Arkansas.

On May 17, 1954, the Supreme Court of the United States declared that the segregation of the races in the public schools is in violation of the Federal Constitution. At the same time the Supreme Court deferred judgment on the questions of time and methods for the accomplishment of integration. *Until the Supreme Court of the United States makes its decision of May 17, 1954, more specific, Little Rock School District will continue with its present program.*

It is our responsibility to comply with Federal Constitutional Requirements and we intend to do so when the Supreme Court of the

United States outlines the method to be followed.

During this interim period we shall do the following:

1. Develop school attendance areas consistent with the location of white and colored pupils with respect to present and future physical facilities in Little Rock School District.

2. Make the necessary revisions in all types of pupil records in order that the transition to an integrated school system may serve the best interests of the entire school district.

3. Make research studies needed for the implementation of a sound school program on an integrated basis.

Little Rock citizens have always been cooperative. They have had the understanding and tolerance required to solve any difficult problem. We solicit your same help and understanding in the creation of an integrated school program required as a result of the Supreme Court Decision.

As I talked, I observed that my audience, which had arrived in high spirits, was rapidly losing its enthusiasm. They knew that the nearby town of Sheridan already had announced it would immediately integrate its schools—in fact, it never did—and they expected Little Rock to do the same.

There were the two editors of the local Negro newspapers in the audience. One of them was C. H. Jones of the *Southern Mediator Journal*, who had helped me arrange the meeting. Jones was not a man to compromise on the issue of civil rights but he had a strong sense of civic responsibility and his newspaper supported our integration plan. The other was L. C. Bates, of the *State Press*, a slender, determined man and a crusading editor. He was also the husband of Mrs. Daisy Bates, the state president of the NAACP. When I had finished my remarks, Bates got to his feet restlessly.

"Then the Board does not intend to integrate the schools in 1954?" he asked.

"No," I replied, "it must be done slowly. For instance, we must complete the additional school buildings that are now being started."

Bates turned abruptly and walked out of the meeting, and later his newspaper was critical of the Board's statement.

The Reverend F. C. Guy, pastor of the largest Negro Baptist church, also made it clear that the meeting was disappointing. He had long been a much respected man, intelligent, sincere and influential in the community. He was an excellent speaker, courteous and calm, and I believe that this was the only occasion on which I ever saw him in danger of losing his composure.

"Next to the law of God," he said, "the Constitution of the United States means the most to me. When you start to tinker with the Constitution of the United States it becomes awfully important to us."

But he did not walk out, nor did anyone else. We talked for three hours and we found solid ground for co-operation.

"A greater responsibility now rests on Negro citizens," I said. "We must approach this problem carefully and sanely. The School Board will not delay merely for delay's sake but to be able to do the job right."

The meeting was important. Some Negro leaders continued to demand greater speed, but in the long struggle ahead we had the co-operation of probably 95 per cent of the Negro citizens, including the Reverend Guy.

II

During the summer school vacation of 1954 I put various members of my staff to work on research projects relating to integration, and I began an intensive poll of public opinion that continued for months. I talked to many hundreds of persons in all walks of life. I attended no less than 225 meetings of all kinds—civic, business, church, social groups as well as white and Negro Parent-Teacher Association sessions at all levels. The integration problem was not always on the agenda during the first months but it was always discussed informally and I spent most of my time listening. I listened to determined segregationists of the Capital Citizens' Council which was affiliated with the White Citizens' Council operations throughout the South. And I listened to leaders of the Urban League, the Council on Human Relations and the NAACP—most of whom favored immediate complete integration.

There was, however, a preponderant body of opinion—*including most Negro citizens*—somewhere in between.

"The decision may be legally and morally right," parents frequently told me, "but the Court should have delayed it until conditions are more favorable in the South. The decision came twenty-five years too soon. Integration will lower the educational standards."

"If we have complete integration," others would say, "my children just won't attend the public schools."

And there were some who said: "I will refuse to support public schools if they are integrated. I'll work through the legislature to abolish public schools and I'll work to eliminate local tax support for public education in the future."

There was a general tendency to denounce Chief Justice Earl Warren and to blame him for the Court's action, although the decision had been unanimous. "What we've got is a Warren-Myrdal court," one man remarked, linking the Chief Justice with the noted Swedish sociologist whose writings were reputed to have influenced him. Many citizens also criticized President Eisenhower (who had won a big vote for a Republican in Little Rock) because he was responsible for appointing Chief Justice Warren.

In general, the people agreed with the School Board that they would have to respect the law, but they hoped enforcement would be delayed. When I was asked specifically what the school authorities were going to do I replied: "I do not consider it to be the job of the school or of the School Board to interpret the law. That is the duty of the courts and the civil authorities. But when the decisions have been made, we have to try to live with the law and also to maintain our educational standards. We can comply with the law if we are given a long period so that we can take small steps in developing and activating a very gradual program of integration that will be acceptable to the large majority in a border state community such as this. I don't believe the Court will insist on haste."

This, of course, proved to be correct when the Court, after new hearings in April of 1955, handed down an implementing decision that called for compliance "with all deliberate speed" and specified that federal district courts would retain jurisdiction over cases before them and check on compliance by local school boards.

Later, in my many talks with various groups in the community about our integration program I emphasized five points I believed we must observe to achieve acceptance of any plan. These were:

1. Each school district should have its own plan of integration specially tailored to meet conditions in that district.

2. We must approach the problem intelligently and not emotionally.

3. We must respect the law.

4. We must make the best instead of the worst of a difficult situation and thus respect the rights of all.

5. We must do everything possible to maintain educational standards and that can be best achieved with the voluntary cooperation of Negro residents in a plan of orderly, gradual integration.

III

In working out a plan for integration I told the School Board and its attorneys that we would have to walk a very tight rope and move one small step at a time. My own staff—particularly Mrs. Macy Paynter, director of attendance and pupil personnel—made steady progress in their research studies. Originally, I had believed that the best plan would be to start integration in the lowest grades of the elementary school. It seemed to me that six-year-old children would be the least concerned about the color of the skin of classmates. They would not have had time to develop strong prejudices or to become traditionalists. They would accept their classmates and, as they progressed from grade to grade, the process of integration would come slowly and naturally over the years.

This plan looked pretty good on paper but, in practice, it was quickly shown to be a complete mistake for us. I first began to realize that it would not work when I talked to groups at the PTA meetings. Almost invariably, the parents who were most outspoken against integration had children in the lowest grades at school. The younger the children, the more violent the parents were in their denunciations of the Court's decision. I began to change my mind about starting integration in the lowest grades—and the correctness of that decision was soon demonstrated by the results of our surveys of the school district.

The surveys showed clearly the difficulty of integrating our elementary schools in 1954. The eastern section of Little Rock had a large Negro population but the percentage of Negroes decreased as you moved toward the center of the city. Then, as you moved west, the percentage of Negro families dwindled until there were almost none. My staff made large maps of the school district and listed the number of white and colored children who were eligible to attend each school. These charts graphically demonstrated that elementary schools in the western part of the city would have only one or two or perhaps no Negroes in the lowest grades but that, in the eastern part of the city, there would be as many as 726 Negro students and only fourteen white students in a single school.

The School Board felt that it would be a great mistake to start integration with an elementary school in which the Negroes outnumbered the white students by a ratio of over fifty to one, and I fully agreed. We then concentrated our research on the senior high school—the tenth, eleventh and twelfth grades. At that time, there was only one high school building for white students and one for Negroes. But two new high schools were being built and both would be opened by 1957. One was Horace Mann High School in the eastern or predominantly Negro area and the other was Hall High School in the northwest or predominantly white area of the city. When these were ready, the old Negro high school would be used as a junior high school, but Central High School would still be used, making three senior high schools.

As a result, we were dividing the city into three new high school attendance areas in which the student population was divided—I will give figures for 1957—as follows:

School	Area	White	1957 Colored	Total
Horace Mann (to be all Negro)	No. 1	426	533	959
Central High (to be integrated)	No. 2	2,135	516	2,651
Hall High (to be all white)	No. 3	700	6	706

As we studied comparable figures in 1954, we began to see how a plan might be worked out for gradual integration of the schools over a period of years—approximately seven years, as finally decided by the federal Court. There were certain factors in our favor, including the construction of two new schools and the fact that the city would henceforth be divided into three areas.

The Horace Mann school, for example, was built to accommodate 1,000 students in Area No. 1. And Central High School could accommodate 2,650 as compared to the 2,135 white students eligible in Area No. 2. We believed, therefore, that the first impact of integration on the community—and I must emphasize that we wanted to minimize that impact—would be lessened by a system of transfers (all transfers would have to be voluntary) of both Negro and white students.

For example, we knew that in view of the circumstances all of the white students in Area No. 1 would desire to transfer to Area No. 2 so they could continue to attend Central High. We believed, correctly, that the six Negro students in Area No. 3 would voluntarily transfer to Horace Mann. The question was whether a large majority of the Negro students in Area No. 2 would transfer to Horace Mann, thus permitting us to start the integration program by having only a few Negro students among the 2,000 attending Central High.

Now, I have no doubt that many integrationists will regard such a plan as an evasion or an unworthy compromise. I can only say that such observers fail to understand the circumstances, as will be amply demonstrated in this book. Our purpose was to comply with the law in a manner that would be accepted locally, not to wreck the school system.

Furthermore, I want to emphasize that when we hoped most of the Negro students in Area No. 2 would voluntarily transfer to the Horace Mann school in the predominantly Negro area we knew what we were talking about. Let me explain. Many segregationists in the South flatly argue that the Negro does not approve of the Supreme Court decision in the Brown case and does not want his children to go to school with white children. I've often heard a woman say: "Why, I talked it over with my colored maid and she said she wouldn't think of letting her children go to a white school."

Well, that kind of argument is ridiculous. Many Negroes do say such things to white employers but for obvious reasons, economic or personal, and not because of their true attitude. Like everybody else, Negro parents want their children accepted and, especially, they want them to have better educational opportunities. Under a segregated system, Negro schools had lagged behind for a variety of reasons, including the fact that Southern states usually spent less money on them than on white schools until recent years. But, if I may digress for a moment, more than just lack of tax money was responsible for lower standards in Negro schools of most Southern states. It has been my experience that there are a limited number of excellent Negro teachers in the

South and a considerable majority of others who do not come up to standard. I have discussed this with many educators in colleges and universities and they often admitted that they required white students seeking degrees in the field of education to meet higher standards than Negro students in the same category.

The attitude of these professors can best be described as one of sympathy toward Negroes because they face certain handicaps in our society. But the result has been unfortunate, because for this and other reasons there has been laxity, particularly in the South, in holding to rigorous standards in training Negro teachers. Thus, there were generally less able teachers and lower educational standards in Negro schools, even when excellent school plants and equipment were provided. The intelligent Negro parents recognized these facts, and Negroes generally welcomed the Supreme Court's integration decision.

There was still more to the picture, however, in a city like Little Rock. I talked to countless Negro leaders, PTA meetings and civic groups while formulating our integration plan and they were well aware of the dangers of immediate and complete integration. They often pointed out that too much haste would almost certainly result in action by the state legislature to abolish public education. They were opposed to rash action for many reasons—fear of economic retaliation, fear of bucking tradition or, in most instances, a sane, reasonable desire to avoid a violent upheaval. There were, of course, some leaders who would continue to demand quick action, but I am convinced that the great majority agreed in principle with the School Board's go-slow policy.

If the reader should believe that I am mistaken in this conviction, let me look ahead for a moment and say that when the time came only about eighty out of several hundred eligible Negro children in Area No. 2 indicated interest in registering at Central High School. We naturally wanted Negro students who were best fitted to adjust themselves to the situation. I asked the principals of the Negro junior and senior high schools to provide me with the names of students who were interested in attending Central High School. After I received their list of about eighty names, I told the principals to talk with these students and their parents about the problems that any child would face in a pilot program of integration.

"In the interests of these children," I added, "I believe you and the teachers who know them best should determine whether they are mentally and emotionally equipped for this transition. Then in your talks with students and parents it should be your purpose to guide those who are not equipped away from participation in the transition program."

In this way, the original number of about eighty was reduced to thirty-two. I then had individual conferences with the thirty-two students and their parents. I had a pupil personnel record for each child and, in these conversations, I relied heavily on the students' mental ability, achievement record, school citizenship record and health record. This was a difficult and often heart-rending experience for me as well as for some of the students.

There was one girl, for example, who knew that her best friend already had been selected. But I reluctantly concluded that this girl lacked the necessary scholastic background and emotional stability.

"You and I are trying to make a decision in the best interest of this child," I told her mother in the girl's presence. "In view of these factors, I recommend that you withdraw her application."

"I believe you're right, Mr. Blossom," the mother said.

The girl's shoulders drooped, big tears came into her eyes and she started sobbing. "Come on, let's go home," the mother said softly, putting her arm around her daughter's shoulders. The girl was still crying as they left.

On another occasion two terrific football players from Horace Mann—both over six feet tall—came to my office to enroll in Central High. They were interested only in football, their scholastic records were below average and I felt it would be a serious mistake for them to transfer.

"You boys want to play football," I told them, "but I must explain that if you were on the Central High School team most of our schedule would be canceled because other schools in our conference are not integrated, and would refuse to play us. Fayetteville, which has some Negroes on its team now, has already had the experience of having games canceled. So you would not only not get to play but you would be depriving others of a chance to play."

The two athletes accepted this in a good spirit. "Mr. Blossom," one of them said, "nobody had explained that to us and we didn't understand the situation."

As a result of this screening process, the number of applications was further reduced to seventeen. I felt that the Negro parents generally exercised good judgment and were highly co-operative in this regard. I repeatedly told them that they had a right to go to Central High because they lived in that attendance area but I believed the school and the parents should focus on what would be best for the child. None of the parents disagreed or protested.

Later, when tension became great just before the opening of school, eight of the seventeen who had been accepted withdrew for reasons of their own, leaving nine to enter the school. This obviously does not mean that other eligible Negro students preferred to attend Horace Mann, but it does mean a heavy majority of Negro residents willingly co-operated with the Board's program of integration.

IV

We completed our research and worked out our plan for integration in detail during the 1954-55 school year. Throughout that period I was constantly presenting our ideas to the public and we were guided in many matters by the reaction of parents and civic leaders. By May, 1955, we believed we were on firm ground despite the objections of some extremists on both sides, and on May 24 the School Board officially adopted what was called the Little Rock

Phase Program for gradual integration. It soon became known popularly or unpopularly as the "Blossom Plan."

All six members of the Board voted for the plan. They were Dr. Cooper, Mrs. Edgar Dixon, Dr. Dale Alford, Harold Engstrom, Jr., R. A. Lile and Mrs. Arthur E. McLean. This should not be taken to mean that members of the Board favored integration. Some, in fact, were very much opposed, including Dr. Alford, but they voted for the plan because the Board's attorneys assured them that it represented a legal minimum of compliance with the law.

Just prior to the opening of school in September, 1955, it became my duty to present and explain the integration plan to the staff of the public schools, about eight hundred in all. I must confess I was a little nervous about this meeting. Many of the teachers were natives of Southern states and I knew they were not at all happy about the prospect of integrating the schools. My nervousness increased when the day of the meeting turned out to be hot and sticky, and there was an air of restlessness in the auditorium as the teachers took their seats.

Furthermore, it took a long time to read and explain the statement of policy which the School Board had approved. I tried to hurry along, but the noon luncheon hour approached and I still was not finished. I kept on talking and getting hotter by the minute and when, at last, I had completed my exposition I was not at all sure whether my audience was thinking about what I had said or thinking about missed luncheons. I was, therefore, very pleasantly surprised when the Board's plan was greeted enthusiastically by the teachers. They applauded loudly and later many of them expressed their satisfaction with the way in which we planned to face the problem of integration.

I think I might add here that the teachers generally were no different in their attitude toward integration from other residents of Little Rock, but all of them did their best to uphold respect for the law.

The integration plan approved by the Board started out by saying that integration could not be accomplished until the school facilities authorized or under construction—particularly two new senior high schools and two new junior high schools—had been completed. The Board also said that integration must wait until the Supreme Court had decided pending cases which would spell out the time to be allowed and the amount of integration to be required.

The statement said that integration should not be attempted simultaneously in all grades but that an "orderly, systematically planned process should be followed."

"In our opinion," it continued, "integration should begin at the high school level, grades ten through twelve. Following successful integration at the senior high school level, it should then be started in the junior high schools. After successful integration in junior and senior high schools it should be started in elementary schools, the third phase of the program. Present indications are that the school year 1957-58 may be the first phase of this program. . . . The time required in the process as outlined should not be construed as unnecessary delay but that which is justly needed with respect to the size and complexity of the job at hand. . . . By starting integration at the senior high school level the process will begin where fewer teachers and students are involved."

In addition to this public statement, a long memorandum was prepared to clarify procedure, particularly in regard to the manner in which pupil transfers would be permitted. The Board's purpose in regard to transfers was to lessen the impact of integration on local cultural patterns by a system of voluntary transfers allowing both white and colored students to maintain, as far as possible, the system of segregated education. The Board restated the principle of "providing the maximum in educational opportunity for all children" and proposed to provide "the necessary safeguards against possible educational loss of attainment for all its school children." This policy was emphasized because it was necessary to offset the sincere belief of many white parents that Negro students, coming from schools with lower educational standards, would drag down the standards of integrated schools.

The Board said that to give each child the best education in the "light of his individual ability and achievement" it would inaugurate a policy of allowing transfers of students from one school area to another upon request of parents or as a result of study of each case and conferences among students, school authorities and parents. This policy enabled any student who was a member of a racial minority in his own school area to transfer to the nearest school in which his own race was in a majority.

"Little Rock School District plans to begin to integrate its schools with a Three Phase Method in order to comply with the Supreme Court decision," the Board's memorandum said. "There are many danger signals on the horizon which should be carefully watched. To move faster could easily result in placing our system of free public education in danger."

A week after the School Board adopted the plan the Supreme Court clarified its 1954 decision and instructed local school boards and federal district courts to integrate the schools at the earliest possible date in the light of local conditions. Our plan called for systematic integration over a period of years and we did not believe it could be attempted safely at any greater speed. On the other hand, if we had had no outside interference and if we had been properly aided by various governmental agencies, I have no doubt that Little Rock's Central High School would have been peacefully integrated in 1957.

Chapter Three

PORTENTS OF

OPPOSITION

DURING THE BUSY PERIOD, starting in the summer of 1954, in which we were formulating our gradual integration plan, there were a number of developments in Arkansas that had a favorable bearing on our problem.

For one thing, Governor Francis A. Cherry, who was seeking re-election, said that the state always had obeyed the law and would continue to obey the law. Orval E. Faubus, who was regarded as a liberal Democrat at that time, was criticized by some for injecting the integration issue into the campaign when he became a candidate for the governorship but he took a moderate position.

"It is evident to me," Faubus said in a formal statement, "that Arkansas is not ready for a complete and sudden mixing of the races in the public schools and that any attempt to solve this problem by pressure or mandatory methods will jeopardize, in many communities, the good relations which exist between whites and Negroes. In my opinion, de-segregation is the No. 1 issue in this gubernatorial campaign and I am therefore making my position clear at the outset with the expressed hope that this issue does not become a temptation to acts and declarations of demagoguery on the part of those who might seek to play upon racial prejudice for selfish ends or, as in the case of communism, to create ill will between whites and Negroes and disrupt this country."

He later said that if elected he would "pledge the facilities of the Governor's office to implement and assist in any way possible the decisions of each local school district in the matter of segregation." He asserted that "gradualism" was the only course the state could follow in bringing about desegregation. When a reporter asked him what the Governor could do about enforcing the will of the local school districts, he said that it "might be necessary to keep down strife" but he declined to say whether he would use the National Guard, if necessary, to support such localities as might oppose integration.

Most political observers believed that Cherry would be reelected but in the last days of the campaign his supporters committed political blunders—in no way connected with integration—and Faubus defeated him. Since Faubus' position was entirely in line with the School Board's policy, this seemed at the time to favor success of our integration program.

I might also mention that after our integration plan was officially adopted and published and had been thoroughly discussed by the newspapers and many public meetings, the *Arkansas Democrat* staged its 1955 popular election of men and women who had contributed most to the progress of Little Rock during the year. In this poll I was chosen Man of the Year in the city on the basis of my work in the schools, which had been largely concerned with drawing up and publicizing the gradual integration plan. In the same election, Winthrop Rockefeller, who had become a cattle breeder in Arkansas and was chairman of the state Industrial Development Board, was named Man of the Year for Arkansas. Rockefeller's support of better opportunity for all was well known.

Such tests of public sentiment seemed to confirm majority support of our plan.

During the late months of 1955 there were, of course, complaints by extremists. Our plan also was criticized by various superintendents of schools in other parts of the state, but I knew that some of them were speaking only because of sentiment in their community and that many of them really approved of our policy. Then, about 5 A.M. on the morning of January 24, 1956, I was awakened by the telephone. My caller said that leaders of the National Association for the Advancement of Colored People had decided to make a legal test of our integration plan and would attempt to register Negro students in every grade later that morning at the opening of the second semester of the school year.

I thanked my informant and went to my office at the usual time. We had anticipated the possibility of some such action and all of the school principals had been instructed to send Negro children to my office if they attempted to register in white schools. About 9:30 A.M. a procession of Negro children and a few parents, accompanied by Mrs. Daisy Bates, state president of the NAACP, and by the Rev. J. J. Crenchaw, arrived at my office.

Mrs. Bates, the wife of the publisher of the *State Press*, was a woman of great energy with an aggressive, crusading spirit. She was an efficient organizer and enjoyed her role as a leading figure in the state's NAACP. I believe I might add that she was not a person about whom others were indifferent. They either approved of her activities or they were highly antagonistic to her, and she was constantly under intense fire of the segregationists. This did not in any way slow her down and sometimes it seemed merely to spur her to greater efforts. For example, she later joined the Central High School PTA, presumably to keep in touch with school activities, although she did not have any children in high school.

On the occasion when she accompanied the children—they were of all ages from first grade to high school—to my office she brought along her own photographer to make a record of the visit. Somebody also had notified the newspapers of the attempt to enroll the Negro children and there was a battery of reporters and photographers on hand.

"These children are here to enroll," Mrs. Bates told me after the crowd had been escorted into my office. "They have already been to the various schools in which they want to enroll and the principals told them to come here. There is one child seeking to enroll in each grade level."

"No," I replied. "I cannot permit such registrations. We are going to follow the School Board's plan of gradual integration."

"Well, may we have a picture taken?" Mrs. Bates asked.

I said I had no objection and the photographic record was made. Then, all smiles, the procession filed out of my office without any protest, since the visit obviously was the preliminary to a legal test of our integration plan. On February 8, Wiley Branton, state chairman of the NAACP Legal Redress Committee, and U. Simpson Tate, a Dallas attorney for the NAACP, filed suit against the School Board, charging that Negro children had been denied admittance to schools solely because of race. This legal action, intended to force a speedup of our plan, was one of the warning signs along the road to 1957. The Negro extremists were dissatisfied. Some of them were citizens of Little Rock but it was obvious that the legal action was being supported, if it had not been initiated, by outsiders.

The legal test by the NAACP was not successful. Judge John E. Miller, in United States District Court, dismissed the suit on the grounds that our plan complied with the Supreme Court order for integration with "all deliberate speed." Branton and Robert Carter, a New York attorney for NAACP, appealed to the Eighth Circuit Court of Appeals in St. Louis and, on April 27, 1957, that court again upheld our plan. The suit was then dropped without explanation, but it seemed likely that the NAACP legal staff came to the conclusion that the Supreme Court also might uphold our plan—and thus establish a legal pattern of gradual integration everywhere.

II

The NAACP legal action to force a speedup in integration was unfortunate from my point of view because, even though it failed, it attracted undesirable attention to the Little Rock situation at a time when calm, intelligent co-operation was essential for the success of our program. Furthermore, the intervention of outsiders in support of the state NAACP was a point not to be ignored by demagogues.

Nevertheless, the net result of the court action probably was to strengthen the majority of Little Rock residents in support of our plan. Except for extremists on both sides, they decided that we had devised a program that conformed to the law and was the best hope of avoiding an upheaval. It represented minimum integration, to be sure, but that was definitely what the majority of white residents wanted. I was frequently complimented by ardent segregationists because they believed our plan was the best they could get without wrecking the school system. The Negro community in general was willing to go along.

There was still another apparently favorable development in this period. Governor Faubus ran for re-election in 1956 and was opposed by Jim Johnson, a rabid segregationist who made school integration the main issue in the campaign. This segregationist attack failed and Faubus was re-elected for a second term, indicating that moderates were in control.

All of these factors increased our optimism, but they were deceptive factors. Trouble was building up behind the scenes. Perhaps "behind the scenes" is misleading because many of the real trouble-makers were far from Little Rock. They were in the strongly segregationist eastern part of the state and in other Southern states and in political circles as far away as Washington.

Extremists on both sides were studying developments at Little Rock and trying to decide whether it would be to their advantage to force a fight-to-the-finish on integration in our city.

For example, Senator James O. Eastland of Mississippi and other Southern segregationist leaders had begun taking pot shots at Faubus. The Senator made clear why attention was centered on our plan.

"In Arkansas, where the Governor will not take action, racial integration has already started," Eastland said in a speech at Tupelo, Mississippi. "The Deep South is all right, but there is now being waged a tremendous conflict in the border states, which will determine what will happen to the Deep South. If the Southern states are picked off one by one under the damnable doctrine of gradualism I don't know if we can hold out or not."

Eastland attacked "weak-kneed politicians at state capitols" in the border states. When Faubus was informed of this speech he chuckled but he also took strong exception to the charge that he had done nothing. He pointed out that two initiated acts would go on the ballot in November aimed at blocking complete integration of public schools in Arkansas, and that he had approved them. One of the measures—an interposition action—was designed to forestall the U.S. Supreme Court decisions from going into effect. The other was the school assignment law, which would authorize the assigning of students to schools and, in effect, send Negro and white students to segregated schools. Both acts, incidentally, were approved by the voters in November, 1956.

About the same time, under pressure of eastern Arkansas politicians, Governor Faubus appointed a committee to go to Virginia and study plans made there for "massive resistance" to school integration. The committee included two influential members from eastern Arkansas—Marvin Bird, chairman of the state Board of Education, and Richard McCulloch, who later became attorney for the State Sovereignty Commission.

After the committee returned, segregationists introduced in the

1957 Legislature four so-called "segregation bills," which were favored by Attorney General Bruce Bennett, who was hopeful of succeeding Faubus as Governor. These bills called for creation of a State Sovereignty Commission to guard state's rights, the removal of the requirement for mandatory school attendance in respect to integrated schools, the registration of individuals and organizations such as the NAACP and the anti-integration Capital Citizens' Council, and authorization for school boards to use school funds to fight integration. Political observers regarded these measures as a kind of political springboard for Bennett, who thereafter worked to create a situation in which Faubus, for reasons of political expediency, would have to approve the bills.

Faubus naturally was not overjoyed by this prospect and he tried to take the position that the segregation bills were not necessary. I talked with him casually several times and was under the impression that he regarded Bennett as an extreme segregationist and did not want him to come into control of the state government. The Governor was, however, subject to some complex political pressures. There are in Arkansas, as in other states, certain powerful business interests that wield strong political influence and often profit by such influence in a perfectly legal manner. These economic interests had opposed Faubus in 1954 but during his first term they changed their tack and, in 1956, strongly supported him. When he was re-elected, they acquired considerable behind-the-scenes political power.

These few men were not necessarily either segregationists or integrationists, but opportunists interested in increasing their power. Demagoguery and bigotry are historical preliminaries to the establishment of arbitrary or dictatorial forms of government and an emotional crisis over racial problems can make a good smoke screen to conceal the maneuvers of men grasping for political control. These men, therefore, were not likely to exert influence on the Governor to prevent or halt an emotional outburst over the school integration issue. The greater the power that accrued to the office of Governor in such a crisis, the stronger the political machine they were building—and the better for them.

Another and probably more important factor was that, in January of 1957, the Legislature also was considering a comprehensive tax program which Faubus very much wanted approved. It was possible for representatives from eastern Arkansas, who were usually able to dominate the Legislature, to block the Governor's tax program unless he accepted the segregation bills. In other words, he honestly and realistically believed he had to do some horse trading to get his tax program. As a result, the Legislature passed the segregation bills and on February 26 the Governor signed them into law. His reluctance, however, was evident when he delayed appointing anyone to the new State Sovereignty Commission until impatient segregationists brought a civil suit against him and forced him to act.

One other development in the spring of 1957 reflected public support of our integration plan. Two new members were to be elected to the School Board on March 16. The White Citizens' Council—spearhead of segregation sentiment in the South—had been showing signs of activity through the Capital Citizens' Council in Little Rock and they came into the open in the School Board election. Robert Ewing Brown, president of the Capital Citizens' Council, and another avowed segregationist, Dr. George P. Branscum, became candidates in opposition to two moderates, Wayne Upton and Henry V. Rath. It was a vicious campaign in which the segregationist organization fired its heavy guns, but the citizens of the city rallied enthusiastically behind Upton and Rath and scored a smashing two-to-one triumph, indicating a powerful moderate majority in the city.

Thus, through the spring of 1957, the bitter-end segregationists had been defeated in every attempt they made to turn the people of Little Rock away from respect for the law of the land, and we had every reason to believe we could smoothly put our "phase" program into effect at the opening of school the following September.

III

One day in the late spring of 1957 a newspaper reporter came to my office.

"Mr. Blossom," he began, "do you really know what's going on in connection with your integration plan?"

"I'm not sure what you mean," I said. "I know there's opposition, but most of the people of Little Rock are behind us."

"Yes," he replied, "but I'm not thinking of just people in Little Rock. I attended a meeting of the Capital Citizens' Council here last night and they're getting ready to shoot the works to stop any kind of integration in the public schools. They've got all kinds of plans, but the first big move will be an all-out attack on you and members of the School Board this summer. They're well organized and they seem to have plenty of money, so you can expect real trouble.

"And don't imagine this is just a local affair. They've got people and backing from eastern Arkansas and other states. There was a preacher from Dallas who spoke last night and, believe me, he was pulling out all the stops on the organ."

Later I read a newspaper account of a speech to the Capital Citizens' Council that said:

Rev. J. A. Lovell of Dallas, a radio minister, advocated "bloodshed if necessary" to prevent racial integration of the schools in a speech to the Capital Citizens' Council last night at the Hotel Lafayette.

Mr. Lovell got his biggest applause from an audience of 250 in his fist-pounding oration when he said:

"If the integration of the races continues while the Supreme Court and other public officials keep their weak-kneed attitude, there are people left yet in the South who love God and their nation enough to shed blood if necessary to stop this work of Satan. We won't take this lying down." Mr. Lovell said violence would be avoided if possible.

He denounced the Supreme Court, Eleanor Roosevelt, the United Nations, Woodrow Wilson, communism and "the hidden hand which is the invisible world government."

He described the United Nations as "that Godless outfit," Eleanor Roosevelt as "that old battle ax," and said the Supreme Court defied any description he could give it.

In adding former President Wilson to the list of recent segregationist targets, the minister said it was in his administration "that we had the start of deceit and hypocrisy."

He said the Bible "is the original book on segregation and God was the original segregationist."

Race mixing, he said, was "a device by Satan to destroy the fertility of the white man's brain."

I knew, of course, that the Capital Citizens' Council in Little Rock, headed by Robert Ewing Brown, was allied with the White Citizens' Councils organization that had been started in Mississippi and spread elsewhere in the South to fight school integration. But I was not fully aware of their activities until they began importing speakers for public meetings and started circulating pamphlets calling on Governor Faubus to use his police powers to prevent integration.

Actually, their campaign of pressure on the Governor had started in April, when Brown wrote him a letter that was to be used as the basis of hundreds of thousand of circulars and many full-page newspaper advertisements. The letter was cleverly worded to mislead the public into believing that our school integration plan had been drawn up or inspired by Northerners and the NAACP. But, most important of all, it asserted that the Governor of Texas has used Texas Rangers to stop integration of a school at Mansfield and that Governor Faubus legally could prevent integration and be "immune" from punishment by the federal courts.

The letter, as later presented to the public in advertisements, said:

RACE-MIXING IN ALL ARKANSAS SCHOOLS
CAN BE STOPPED BY THE GOVERNOR

HOW? Read solution below by President of the Capital Citizens'
Council in letter to the Governor April 30, 1957

To: Governor Orval E. Faubus
     Little Rock, Arkansas   1131465

The people of Pulaski County and the State of Arkansas expressed
themselves last November when they approved overwhelmingly the . . .
segregation proposals on the ballot.

The 1957 legislature, with your help, followed the will of the people
by passing four segregation laws.

The Little Rock School Board, dominated by its superintendent, who
was born, reared and educated just below the Iowa state line in Northwest Missouri, announced a school race-mixing policy one week after
the federal Supreme Court's May 17, 1954, opinion.

The school board and the superintendent played along with the
NAACP and wound up in federal court on the question of should
we mix completely now, or just start with the high schools.

In Clinton, Tennessee, there were only 12 Negroes to mix; in Mansfield, Texas, only 13; in Hoxie, Arkansas, only 25 (of which only 6
are still in school). But in Little Rock, 30 per cent of the pupils are
Negro. The superintendent says that 200 are to go to the white Central
High School in September.

*Under the sovereignty of the State of Arkansas, you can, under our
police powers, in order to preserve domestic tranquility, order the two
races to attend their own schools. As the sovereign head of a state, you
are immune to federal court orders.*

Mansfield, Texas, was ordered by a federal judge to admit 13 Negroes,
but when trouble started, the governor sent Texas Rangers there, and
ordered the 13 Negroes back to their schools. That was the end of the
trouble.

The Central High School here in Little Rock is 30 years old. The tax-
payers, less than 2 years ago, opened the million dollar Horace Mann
Negro high school. It is not overcrowded. Just why do Negroes need
to go to our white high school?

Governor, as executive head of this state, please act forthrightly, because the problem will not go away unless you solve it. An ounce of prevention is still worth a pound of cure. You, Governor, and you alone, can act on this most serious matter—will you?

Respectfully, Robert Ewing Brown, President
Capital Citizens' Council

THE CAPITAL CITIZENS' COUNCIL MAINTAINS THAT:

1. Since a sovereign state is immune to federal court orders . . .
2. Since the Governor as head of the sovereign state is also immune to federal court orders . . .
3. Since the Governor, himself, placed on the ballot in last November's general election a resolution of interposition calling for the use of these sovereign powers to protect our people . . .
4. Since the people of Arkansas by a tremendous, overwhelming majority approved the Governor's resolution for this purpose . . .
5. Since the legislature backed up the people by voting overwhelmingly and passing four segregation laws . . .

THE GOVERNOR SHOULD EXERCISE THIS SOVEREIGNTY TO PROTECT THE PEOPLE OF ARKANSAS

HE WAS ELECTED ON THIS BASIS

WIRE, WRITE OR PHONE THE GOVERNOR . . . URGE HIM TO USE THESE POWERS NOW

Brown's letter to Faubus was designed to put Faubus "on the spot" as the man who held the key to success or failure of our integration plan. But the Governor had no desire to accept that role. In fact, he told a press conference on July 17 that he hadn't read the Capital Citizens' Council's flamboyant advertisements. He referred to the segregation bills passed by the 1957 Legislature but added, significantly, that "everyone knows no state law supersedes a federal law. If anyone expects me to try to use them to supersede federal laws they are wrong."

The segregationist leaders, however, did not intend to let him avoid responsibility, and they appealed directly to the people in a gigantic propaganda campaign. Die-hard segregationists from all over the South began concentrating money and talent to arouse public sentiment and force a showdown in our city on the theory that if integration could be stopped there it would not be their problem for a long time. There was no longer any doubt that they were out for the kill.

Pressure on the Governor was being intensified. Amis Guthridge, a director of the Capital Citizens' Council, went over into Oklahoma to carry the word. He bitterly attacked Faubus as a "do-nothing Governor on the segregation issue" and, picking up an old frontier phrase, said: "There'll be hell on the border if they try to integrate at Little Rock in September!"

And, unhappily, he was right.

Chapter Four

EXTREMISTS BEAT A

PATH TO LITTLE ROCK

IN THE SPRING of 1957 I had been confident that our carefully prepared plan for gradual integration of the public schools at Little Rock would prove successful. Several Arkansas schools already were integrated. At Fayetteville, the few Negro students eligible were absorbed into the high school without creating any problems. At Hoxie, a small town in eastern Arkansas, the School Board integrated approximately twenty-five Negro children into the white schools. When segregationists demonstrated against integration, the School Board itself went into federal court and secured what has since become known as the "Hoxie type" restraining injunction against interference. The demonstrations ceased and school integration proceeded. Much later, a petition for recall of certain School Board members was defeated by the voters of Hoxie.

There had been no reason in the spring of 1957 to believe that the Little Rock integration plan would be any less successful. But by midsummer our plan was under a vicious, massive attack by segregationists from all over the South and I was the main target.

The attempts at character assassination and distortion of fact as practiced by the extreme segregationists were many and varied. Let me cite one incident that had its beginning in the appearance of Amis Guthridge and the Reverend Wesley Pruden, Sr., pastor of a small Baptist church in a local residential development, before a public meeting of the School Board.

The School Board customarily met in the conference room at the school administration building in the business district. After integration became an issue, the segregationists regularly rounded up a large group to attend public meetings of the Board and the room was usually filled to overflowing. They also always notified the newspapers when they planned to make an attack on our integration plan and we had reporters and photographers added to the crowd. The Board's policy was to allow time for members of the audience to express their views or to make suggestions on any subject that was up for consideration. Occasionally, questions were asked by Negro citizens or ideas were advanced. But, in the summer of 1957, we could be confident that members of the Capital Citizens' Council or some other segregationist group would tear into the Board, often in a highly emotional burst of oratory, at every meeting.

Once, after such a session, I left the building with a Board member who was strongly in favor of segregation in the schools but was getting fed up with the antics of the Capital Citizens' Council. "When I have to go through meetings like this one," he said, "it almost makes me an integrationist."

Guthridge and the Reverend Pruden were frequent spokesmen for the segregationists at the School Board meetings. The Baptist pastor had not been widely known in Little Rock but he played a prominent role in the segregationist campaign. He was heavy-set, with thinning curly hair. He dressed well and was a determined speaker, positive in manner and with a remarkable ability to restrain his emotions. I never saw him lose his temper and I thought that he was likely to give his audience an impression of coldness and calculation in his approach to almost any subject. But he was persuasive and aggressive and a dangerous opponent.

Guthridge was quite a different type. Tall, with glasses and thin hair, he was a good talker although usually emotional when he was on a subject in which he believed sincerely, as he did believe sincerely in segregation. He gave me the impression that he believed the world would come to an end if the Little Rock schools were integrated. He had once dealt in sale of office furniture and he still had an antique shop, but he was also a lawyer. In my opinion, he was frequently inclined to exaggeration and carelessness with facts when arguing against our plan for school integration.

On the evening I mentioned—one of his many appearances before the School Board—Guthridge said he represented the parents of certain schoolchildren and he demanded that the Board establish separate schools for white children who did not wish to attend integrated schools.

"I am asking you not to attempt any compulsory integration in this district," he said. He then switched to attack on "a certain newspaper editor"—presumably Harry S. Ashmore, executive editor of the *Gazette*—as "a self-appointed oracle on the race question" who had misled the people regarding integration.

Mr. Pruden asked the Board various questions about how integration would affect social and other school activities. The American Baptist Association, incidentally, at a Little Rock meeting of three thousand delegates from all over the country in 1956, had adopted a strongly worded resolution endorsing segregation in all walks of life.

The Board suggested that both Guthridge and Pruden put their requests in writing. Later I received a letter from Mr. Pruden but, even before I had time to open it, the contents were being reprinted in big newspaper advertisements under sponsorship of the Citizens' Council. The advertisement, in part, is reprinted below with my answers—which were written later—inserted in italics:

Virgil Blossom & Little Rock School Board

SPEAK UP SO WE CAN HEAR YOU!!!

A prominent Little Rock minister has asked you publicly the following questions about your race-mixing plans. Come out in the open and let us know in plain words what you are planning to do with our children!

WHEN YOU START RACE MIXING—WHERE ARE YOU GOING TO STOP?

The ministers' questions: —

Question 1: "If you integrate Little Rock Central High in September will the negro boys and girls be permitted to attend the school sponsored dances? Would the negro boys be permitted to solicit the white girls for dances? Or would discrimination be permitted here?"

Answer: Certain social functions of our schools which have been desirable in the past may have to be eliminated. (Social functions which would involve race mixing will not be held.)

Question 2: "Will the white girls be forced to take their showers with the negro girls, using the same facilities, in connection with their gym classes? Or will discrimination be permitted here?"

Answer: All boys and girls will use the regular facilities provided in required school programs.

Question 3: "If you integrate our Central High School in September, will that not automatically integrate the white and colored mothers of the school sponsored PTA? Will the negro women be permitted to hold office and serve as committee chairmen? Or will discrimination be permitted here?"

Answer: The Parent-Teacher Association is a voluntary organization of adults which is self-governing in nature (not controlled by the Board of Education or School Administration). They form their own policies, elect or select on a democratic majority-rule basis their officers and committee chairmen. The parents who have made up this organization in the past have handled many difficult problems in a commendable manner. *In view of their past actions we have confidence in them on any problem which may confront them in this matter.*

Question 4: "Will the negro boys and girls be allowed to join the school sponsored clubs that the children belong to? When out-of-town trips are taken by these club children will the negro boys and girls be permitted to go along? Will they stay in the same motels, hotels or private homes with the white children? Or will discrimination be permitted here?"

Answer: The Board of Education authorizes from time to time, on an individual basis, grade-level social clubs, formed and supervised by parents in co-operation with the school faculty. Mixing of the races need not take place in these organizations as they are not a required part of the school program.

On school club trips, particular care has always been taken for the welfare of each child. The selection of the pupils making the trip, choice of chaperones, housing arrangements, and the conduct of the pupils have always been subject to the best judgment of the school authorities. The selections have been in harmony with social customs acceptable to our patrons and in the community to be visited. (These policies will be continued.)

Question 5: "Because of the high venereal disease rate among negroes, the Public is wondering if the white children will be forced to use the same rest rooms and toilet facilities with negroes? Or will discrimination be permitted here?"

Answer: School facilities will be used by all pupils in the regular school program. Board of Education policy requires the immediate exclusion from school of any pupil having an infectious or contagious disease. Readmission to school is based on a doctor's certificate stating that the pupil is free from infectious or contagious disease.

Question 6: "Integration will throw white and negro children together in the dramatic classes. When the script calls for the enactment of tender love scenes, will these parts be assigned to negro boys and white girls without respect to race or color? Or will discrimination be permitted here? Since the integrationists so stoutly maintain there is no basic difference in the races, it is only natural that the Public is wondering about these things."

Answer: Board of Education policy is such that the situation pictured in this question cannot arise. (*Teachers can, and will, avoid any such problem.*)

Question 7: "If the court should rule that negroes can force their way into the social lives of our children, would the School Board and Superintendent aid and abet the negroes in this matter, or would they stand behind the white people?"

Answer: *It is unwise to make projections on matters which do not exist. (Social functions which would involve race mixing will not be held.)*

LAWYERS TO WHOM WE HAVE SUBMITTED THESE QUESTIONS AGREE THAT ONCE NEGROES ARE ADMITTED AS STUDENTS ANY DISCRIMINATION LISTED ABOVE WILL BE ILLEGAL

JOIN HANDS WITH US, YOUR NEIGHBORS IN THE CITIZENS COUNCIL, AND HELP STOP IT!

This advertisement, using the name of a minister, was highly damaging to the cause of peaceful integration. At the Board's request, I later answered Mr. Pruden's questions as shown in the answers I have inserted above, but the damage had already been done.

The Board also answered Guthridge's request by letter and at the same time issued a formal statement explaining its legal position, as prepared by its attorneys. In effect, this statement said that the new state constitutional amendment and four segregation laws adopted by the 1957 General Assembly did not make it unnecessary for the School Board to comply with the Supreme Court decisions—as the segregationists had argued. The Board invited the segregationists to file a suit in federal court in order to obtain a definite judicial decision, if they desired. But without such a decision, the Board said it would be subject to contempt charges and to serious liabilities if it attempted, as Guthridge had suggested, to establish separate schools for white children who did not wish to enter integrated schools or otherwise to avoid carrying out the gradual integration plan as approved by the federal courts.

The statement said that the Board did not approve of the

principle involved in the Supreme Court decisions but that it had "a duty to obey." State laws, it added, must give way to federal laws and "in our opinion, this language is unmistakable [in the Constitution] and those who say state laws permitting segregation are supreme simply refuse to read that which is plainly written.

"We have confidence in the calm, good judgment and fairness of the citizens of Little Rock. They will understand the difficulties of our position. It is not a question of whether they find the decision of the Supreme Court of the United States agreeable. It is the more serious question of whether they will insist that we violate our oaths as citizens of America and Arkansas by attempting to disobey the decree of the United States District Court.

"We appeal to all citizens to help us solve this problem with temperate and prayerful consideration in the interest of all students."

II

Sitting at my desk and reading newspaper accounts of the activities and defiant words of avid segregationists, I could not escape a weird and ominous feeling as if I were being drawn into some tragic era of the past. I recalled the calculated intolerance with which the Bolshevik minority purged Russia of political moderates. I remembered the hysteria and racial bigotry that marked destruction of democratic processes and the seizure of dictatorial power by a Nazi minority in Germany. But then I looked out the window at the peaceful, prosperous, enlightened city of Little Rock on a pleasant summer day in 1957. I knew the people in the offices and the homes. I knew they were reasonable and law-abiding, and my ominous thoughts faded like a wisp of fog in the warm sunshine. "Yes," I told myself confidently, "those things happened long ago and far away—they can't happen here."

But the fireworks had not really started. In a campaign that went on for months, I was denounced at meetings by demagogues imported from other states. I was derided in pamphlets and leaflets filled with hate propaganda and circulated throughout the state. I was bombarded by letters and telephone calls designed to intimidate me.

Segregationist newspapers outside Little Rock carried on the drive with editorials attacking me as a "carpet-bagger" from the North—I was born in north central Missouri—and as "a confirmed follower or disciple of the National Association for the Advancement of Colored People." "Certainly it would not be beyond the bounds of reason to suppose that he is a paid agent of this organization," the Monroe (Louisiana) *Morning World* said in summing up the segregationist estimate of me several months later. "The people of Little Rock discovered to their dismay that the superintendent of schools was an imported integrationist and that the six members of the School Board were either integrationists or so controlled by Blossom that they were ineffective.

"It was Blossom, and not the federal government, the U.S. Supreme Court, nor the federal district court in which Little Rock is located, who instigated integration. . . . It was Blossom and not the Negroes who actually instigated the idea of placing Negroes in that school."

That is only a sample of the kind of attack that went on week after week. Advertisements and leaflets proclaimed that "White children have rights, too!" and went on to say that I was guilty of gross discrimination against white children because they were "given no choice at all" as to which school they would attend, whereas Negro children were "freely given their choice" as to schools. "Parents," these appeals to prejudice said, "the Blossom race-mixing plan denies us [our] legal rights. . . . FATHERS, MOTHERS, read this carefully! Under the law you do not have to send your children to Central High School if Blossom race-mixes that school. You can require the School Board to give your child equal education benefits elsewhere!"

Pounded steadily by such propaganda, it was little wonder that many persons became confused, and with confusion came uncertainty and fear. At first, the School Board and I attempted to answer the published misrepresentations but, like denials of an evil rumor, the truth can seldom catch up with the original lie and the end result often is merely to spread the rumor more widely. Eventually, we ceased trying to catch up with misrepresentations and made public statements only when absolutely necessary.

During the summer, letters, telegrams and telephone calls from political personages in eastern Arkansas and other Southern states rained down on the Governor's office as a result of a costly and well-organized pressure campaign. Leaflets were everywhere urging citizens to write to the Governor, and the same appeal was repeated in newspaper advertisements that distorted the facts. For example:

THE PEOPLE OF ARKANSAS VS. RACE-MIXING

Official policy of the state of Arkansas: . . . the power to operate the public schools . . . on a racially separate but substantially equal basis was granted by the people of Arkansas to the government. . . .

Where does the Governor stand?

Governor Faubus told us last year that if we supported his segregation measures, no school district in Arkansas would be forced to race-mix against its will. . . . Now Little Rock, North Little Rock, Fort Smith, Van Buren and other places have been ordered by courts to race-mix or have been betrayed into a race-mixing policy by gerrymandered school boards, subservient to an integrationist school lobby. . . . When will the Governor speak?

As Governor he can exercise our sovereignty to protect our people.

Governor Faubus was a man with political knowledge, as well as political ambitions. He had no difficulty looking ahead to 1958, when he wanted a say as to who would be the next Governor. He may or may not have hoped then to be the second man in history to serve three consecutive terms as Governor of Arkansas. In any event, it was only natural that he was keenly aware of the forces behind the segregationist campaign in Little Rock, the powerful political influence of eastern Arkansas and of other Southern states. He was also aware that various state and federal officials were running away from the unpopular duty of enforcing the Supreme Court orders.

As the summer vacation drew toward an end and the opening of school approached, I began to feel that all of the segregationists of the South were beating a path to Little Rock. What we had hoped would be strictly a school administrative matter now was in danger of becoming a political atom bomb that might explode as loudly in Washington as in Little Rock.

One day in August I picked up the newspapers and learned that a Mothers League of Central High School had been formed to oppose integration. Mrs. O. R. Aaron, president, told the first meeting of about one hundred persons that the group was opposed to violence and would work "as a group of Christian mothers in a Christian-like way."

The Mothers League was a highly effective attempt to convince the people that segregationist activities were of a nonviolent character—the League was a symbol of peaceful assembly—and that only legal opposition was contemplated. The Mothers League officers and members attended various meetings of the School Board, seeking delay or changes in our plan.

We emphasized to them that the School Board had no choice but to carry out the law, and we tried to persuade them that our gradual plan of integration was best for the community under the circumstances. We didn't get very far, however, and they later appealed to Faubus to take action on the grounds that they had "exhausted" efforts to discuss the problem with me. The Governor told them he believed the School Board had acted "under duress" when it adopted our integration plan and that he was under the impression a majority of people opposed desegregation. But he did not commit himself, saying that he "must exercise [his] own best judgment" as the occasion arose.

At one meeting of the Mothers League, W. R. Hughes of Dallas, chairman of the executive committee of the Association of Citizens' Councils of Texas, told the women that Communism was "behind every effort of the NAACP" and that "a nigger in your school is a potential Communist in your school. . . . Stand up and fight for your children and never cease as long as you can breathe." On another occasion, an unidentified man stood up in a Mothers League meeting and asked how many persons would gather at Central High when school opened to "push back" any Negroes who tried to enter. "And I imagine there are a few shotguns in Little Rock, too," he added, but he was greeted with silence and a few moans, and the presiding officer rebuked him.

Thus the atmosphere of hysteria grew and there came to me once more that ominous feeling that we were drifting despairingly into another time and another place where normal, reasonable people were so distracted by demagoguery that they were unable to realize until it was too late that they were surrendering dictatorial power to an extremist minority. But, again, I knew that it couldn't happen here in the city of Little Rock. These people were not sheep, to be swayed by the first cry of panic. All that was needed was a single gesture of firm and courageous leadership in behalf of law and order—and the danger of violence would be gone.

Where that leadership would have to originate was now obvious. The integration of Central High School was no longer a local, school administrative problem. The segregationist leaders had succeeded in their strategy of building it into a state political problem, with repercussions throughout the nation. Governor Faubus had wavered and faltered under segregationist pressure and had been maneuvered into a political corner. Now he was the key man and he had to choose. Would he speak out in support of law and order and democratic processes? Would he call out the National Guard if necessary to protect Negro students?—or to prevent integration?

Where does the Governor stand? the segregationists had demanded again and again. Now, the School Board also wanted the answer.

III

After discussing the overall situation at one of our numerous meetings early in August, the president of the School Board, Dr. Cooper, asked me to talk to Faubus, to Federal Judge John E. Miller, who then had jurisdiction over integration at Little Rock, and to Police Chief Marvin Potts. It was the opinion of the Board that the greatest danger to our plans came from die-hard segregationists outside the city. They had decided they must stop our plan just because it was so reasonable and initially involved so few Negro students that it had every chance of success. Their strategy was to prevent at any cost a demonstration that school integration could be accomplished gradually and successfully. I had heard the attitude of segregationist leaders from other cities expressed again and again, in words like these: "If the Little Rock integration plan succeeds, we will be next." And they were determined not to "be next."

In view of this situation, the School Board wanted to know what local, state and federal officials were prepared to do to preserve law and order if trouble arose at Central High School.

I conferred with Police Chief Potts and asked him whether the city police would be prepared for emergency action if necessary. Although Potts obviously was opposed to desegregation, he was a man of integrity and he took his oath of office seriously.

"I'll carry out my oath," he told me. "The police will protect life and property and preserve the peace. Don't worry about that. But let me make clear that I do not regard it as my job to integrate the schools."

I knew Potts would live up to his words. In fact, he and I later conferred with the parents of Negro students, worked out routes by which they could get to Central High School under full police protection, and arranged for all adult Negroes to remain away from that vicinity on the opening day of school. "It takes two sides to start a fight," Potts said, "and if there are no Negro bystanders my job will be a hundred times easier." The Negro leaders agreed with him and there is little doubt that this arrangement—for which Potts deserves full credit—was the only thing that prevented a race riot on the first day of school.

My conference with Judge Miller in his offices at Fort Smith was for the purpose of asking him to issue a public statement that he would tolerate no interference with peaceful implementation of the gradual integration plan which his court had approved. Tall, white-haired and dignified, the Judge obviously did not enjoy his role in the integration conflict. He was sympathetic but he declined to issue any general warning, saying he would deal with problems as they arose.

My most important assignment, of course, was to talk to Governor Faubus. He is a remarkable man in many ways, pleasant, forceful, clever and ambitious. He is distinguished looking, too, with dark hair drawn smoothly back from a high forehead, a wide mouth, deep-set eyes and firm chin. Faubus had been born in a cabin in the Ozark Mountains in northwest Arkansas, and as a boy he worked much of the time with an axe alongside his father in the hickory woods. He graduated from a one-room grammar school at the age of eighteen and then was first among fifty persons taking examinations for a third-grade teacher's license. He taught country school and attended high school part time at Huntsville until he got his diploma at the age of twenty-seven, at which time he had been married for six years.

Sometimes during school vacations, Faubus and his wife were migrant workers picking berries and fruit from Louisiana to Missouri. One summer he worked in the logging camps in Washington state. In 1937, he ran for the state Legislature and was defeated. But he had a liking for politics and a real knack for making friends. He could act or talk like a hillbilly and often did when campaigning in the backwoods. But he also knew how to make the most of his opportunities. He learned quickly and he grew, and he could talk like a schoolteacher or a senator when the occasion demanded. He was elected recorder of Madison County. He served well in France during World War II, and emerged as a major. He became postmaster and owner of the Madison County *Record* after the war and was such a crusading editor that Governor McMath appointed him state highway commissioner and, later, administrative assistant to the Governor. In 1954, he amazed everybody by tramping—often hitch-hiking—day after day through the backwoods, drawling his ideas and pleas for support to the farmers—and getting himself elected Governor.

As Governor, Faubus was willing at times to stick his neck out in a courageous manner. He advocated a big but necessary tax program and he did a great deal to improve the state public education system. He appointed Negroes to positions never before held by members of their race and he furthered integration generally. He also made friends. When elected, Faubus was not popular in Little Rock and he knew it. Not long afterward the Governor was invited, as usual, to join the city's annual "Good Will Train" expedition designed to sell Little Rock as a business center to other cities and towns in the state. When he got on the train, I doubt if Faubus had a real friend in the party. But he worked hard at winning friends during that trip, and when we got back to Little Rock I'm pretty sure that he no longer had an enemy in the entire party.

He could project himself to the public and inspire confidence. He knew how, in one way or another, to handle a difficult or slippery situation. He knew, too, how to picture himself as the underdog, how to gain sympathy for himself as a fighter facing great odds, presumably in behalf of the common people. He played the role well, and it would be important to him in the days to come.

I had known Faubus for years at Fayetteville and I often chatted with him there and in Little Rock. But I was not in a confident mood when I went to the spacious capitol building, set back in beautiful grounds at the head of Capitol Avenue. The Governor was pleasant enough when I was escorted into his office, but I imagined he was keenly feeling the political pressure of the segregationist campaign.

I explained to him that the School Board was concerned that extremists, particularly those from other cities in Arkansas, might cause trouble at the opening of school on September 3. If he would issue a public statement urging respect for the law and saying the state government would not tolerate any kind of violence at Central High School, I added, we believed the outside threats of interference would die away and all would be well.

In this and several later talks I had with Faubus, his replies can best be described as evasive. In the course of these various conversations, at some of which other persons were present, the Governor expressed the opinion that the integration plan worked out by the School Board was the best he had heard of. He said he was certain it would work if only the state's recently-passed segregation laws were declared invalid, and expressed the opinion that they eventually would be. But, meantime, he was in a difficult situation.

"You are aware of my position," he said on several occasions. "I allowed the segregation acts to be introduced into the Legislature and later signed them. Thus, by my actions, I helped make them become state law."

The Governor also referred to the fact that he had appointed a committee to study the "massive resistance" laws—later outlawed by the courts—being framed at that time in Virginia, and, significantly, he said he had a basic commitment and obligation to use state law to delay or prevent integration. I assumed his commitments were political in nature, although he did not express it that way, and that they had grown out of a "horse trade" he had been forced to make to get eastern Arkansas legislators to support his tax program in 1957.

"I implore you," I said on several occasions, "to do nothing that would cause the Little Rock School District to lose its court-approved plan of school integration."

I also told him, as I had told the police, of a conversation I had had some time earlier with Amis Guthridge. Guthridge said there was a group of segregationists who would not join the White Citizens' Council because the Council acted legally and constitutionally, but this group said they would, at the proper time, "take over" with guns and pistols. I asked Guthridge to give me names of persons in this group but he did not.

After one long talk with Faubus, I finally asked: "Governor, just what *are* you going to do in regard to the Little Rock integration plan?"

He thought about the question for a minute before he replied.

"When you tell me what the federals are going to do," he finally answered, "then I will tell you what I am going to do."

I got no more from him in our talks except that I felt he wanted the federal government to act and thus relieve him of responsibility for enforcing integration. I also came away with the impression he feared the political results of aiding integration even to the extent of preserving law and order. Later, I reported to the School Board: "We know where we stand with the city police and Judge Miller. But the Governor is unpredictable. I don't know what he will do."

I suggested that the Board or its officers should talk to Faubus and on August 15 Wayne Upton, secretary of the Board, and I met with him at the Governor's mansion. We got no better results, except that the Governor repeated his belief that our plan would work if only the courts held the state segregation acts invalid. This, he seemed to believe, would persuade the segregationists that all legal means of resistance had been exhausted and presumably would relieve him of his commitments. He suggested that we arrange for a court suit testing the validity of the acts.

"The Board is under court orders and cannot seek any delay," we replied. But we offered to consider his suggestion and we felt that if we arranged for a test suit the Governor would co-operate with us and, if necessary, issue the statement we wanted. Actually, a test suit was filed the next day by William F. Rector, an insurance man, but it seemed to have no effect on Faubus' attitude and was soon lost in the shuffle.

IV

The biggest and most effective blow was struck by the Citizens' Council of Arkansas when it invited Governor Marvin Griffin of Georgia, one of the South's most ardent segregationist leaders, to be the guest of honor at a $10-a-plate dinner at the Hotel Marion in Little Rock on August 22. The Council obviously wanted Griffin not only to stir up maximum public prejudice in Little Rock but particularly to put the final ounce of pressure on Faubus. Griffin, on the other hand, may or may not have seen an opportunity to make a "fall guy" out of Faubus by pushing him into defiance of the federal government—and thus delay a showdown on integration in Georgia.

In any event, Faubus told me he wished Griffin would stay home because he could "only muddy the issue."

"Didn't you ask him to come here?" I inquired.

"No," the Governor said. "I didn't talk to him and I don't know whether I should entertain him while he's here."

"Why don't you telephone and ask him to stay away?"

"I'll think about it," Faubus said.

He did call Griffin and reportedly told him the situation in Arkansas was difficult and that he hoped none of the avid Georgia segregationists accompanying the party would make inflammatory remarks. But Griffin arrived in Little Rock on schedule in a Georgia National Guard airplane and was put up at the Governor's guest house—a fact that he emphasized repeatedly in his public remarks.

Faubus did not attend the dinner for the Georgia Governor because of a previous engagement, but he had breakfast with him the next morning.

Griffin spoke to about three hundred diners, many from out of town, and was frequently interrupted by cheers and rebel yells. He attacked the Supreme Court as having attempted "by naked force to destroy our government itself." He urged the South to resist integration by every legal means and to back a great national propaganda campaign to support "the correctness of our stand and our way of life." He praised "this courageous group of Arkansas patriots who are fighting a dedicated battle to preserve the rights of states." There was much, much more along that line, but his main purpose was to say that Georgia had a formula for legally stopping integration of schools—thus implying that the Arkansas state government could also legally halt integration.

Actually, the implication was incorrect. Griffin pointed out that Georgia had set up legal machinery to provide grants on an equal basis to citizens so they could educate their own children and prevent tax funds being used to operate mixed schools. These grants, he said, would provide for education in each school district "if, as and when the federal government prohibits the operation of our schools. We won't close the schools. They will be closed by court order. If the public schools in Georgia are destroyed, the onus will be on the federal court and not on the people or the state of Georgia. . . . It is a time for courageous action."

In Arkansas there was no such legal machinery and the Governor did not have any power to close the schools at that time and he did not want to close them any more than Griffin wanted to use his power to close schools in Georgia. Yet, Griffin's visit was tremendously effective in behalf of the segregationists. For one thing, a member of Griffin's party, Roy V. Harris, a publisher, also spoke to the diners, and he lived up to Faubus' fears of unbridled oratory. Harris said he believed the nation could be convinced that "our way of life is constitutional, American, Christian and scientific."

He said that "for twenty years the Communists and Reds have conducted a brainwashing campaign through the churches, the two political parties and national organizations, and have been so successful that many people now believe segregation is unconstitutional, un-American, un-Christian and unscientific."

But more important in the long run was the effect of Griffin's visit on Faubus and on public sentiment. The School Board immediately found that it was more difficult to deal with the Governor, and on one occasion he told me that Griffin's speech had done more than "anything else that has happened to solidify public sentiment against school integration." He added that since the Georgia Governor had impressed on the public mind that Georgia wasn't integrating he had been deluged with letters and telegrams saying:

"If Georgia doesn't have any integration plan, why should we?"

That weekend an eight-foot-high fiery cross was burned in front of the home of the state president of the NAACP and a sign found nearby said:

Go back to Africa—KKK

Chapter Five

THE GOVERNOR MAKES HIS CHOICE

ON SUNDAY, August 24, nine days before school opened, about five hundred Negroes gathered in the Dunbar Community Center at Little Rock to hear ministers, teachers, doctors and lawyers discuss preparations for integration of Central High School. The Negro students who already had been screened by my office as the first Negroes eligible to attend the school were present, most of them accompanied by their parents.

The Negro speakers discussed all phases of good citizenship and the responsibilities of the students, from scholarship to hygiene, and impressed upon the audience the importance that would be attached to the conduct of the Negro community generally in the next few weeks. It was a constructive meeting and probably did much to lessen the danger of emotional outbreaks during the integration crisis.

On the other hand, there were developments about the same time that added to the troubles of the School Board, sometimes by intent and sometimes by unfortunate blunders. News coverage of

57

events in Little Rock was a difficult job, and I believe most of the scores of reporters on the scene then and later told as honestly as possible what was happening. But the newsmen naturally wrote mostly about the sensational developments—sometimes making minor incidents into sensations—and the newspaper headline writers did the same in bigger type, so that the net result was to add to the public feeling of hysteria as well as to increase our problems.

At one press conference, for example, the reporters asked me to explain how the Negro students would be introduced to the school.

"Why, just as any new student is introduced," I said. "Members of the student council will show all new students around, explain to them about the luncheon periods in the cafeteria and so on."

The reporter for the Associated Press wrote an accurate story about this, but it was—with no malicious intent—carried on the wire all over the area under the heading:

BLOSSOM SETS UP BUDDY SYSTEM
BETWEEN WHITE AND COLORED STUDENTS

I don't believe any article written about the Little Rock crisis caused Southerners to react more strongly or unintentionally caused me more trouble.

The more the tension mounted late in August the more anxious the School Board was to persuade Governor Faubus to issue a formal statement. At this time, former governor Sidney McMath, who had been Faubus' mentor a few years earlier when he first came into political prominence, was quietly directing a "pressure" campaign in which liberal and moderate political figures in Arkansas and elsewhere were trying to offset the influence of the avid segregationists. They did not make open appeals to the public, but quietly sought to encourage the people of Little Rock and Arkansas to respect the Supreme Court decisions and to refuse support to the extremists. "I think," McMath said later, "that we were able to hold back Faubus supporters and race extremists from capturing any great number of middle-of-the roaders who were off balance because unexpected developments came so quickly."

Faubus himself said in a speech in Louisiana much later that some "Democratic friends urged me to integrate in Little Rock, dangling before me the Vice-Presidency." But he didn't name the "Democratic friends" or accept their advice. He was as vague as ever on August 26 when he met with the entire School Board and Attorney A. F. House—just a week before school opened.

Dr. Cooper, president of the Board, explained that we were not worried about the people of Little Rock causing violence but that we felt the need for support of the state government in event outsiders caused any trouble. "Will you," he asked, "issue a public statement that you will use state forces to uphold law and order, if necessary?"

The Governor said that he did not know if he would issue such a statement because he felt that there should be a delay—that more time was needed before integration was initiated.

"How can there be a delay?" House asked. "We are under order of the Court and if we delay we will be in contempt of court."

"If a state court suit were started," Faubus said, "it would mean delay. The School Board could go into the state court and seek further delay."

In this exchange, Faubus also remarked that the Board and the School Superintendent were "protected"—presumably from political or public retaliation—by the fact that they were acting under court order, but that he had no such protection.

House replied that the Board wanted to co-operate in any legitimate way, but he added: "Under no circumstances will the Board enter into collusion with a state agency to counteract the federal court order. And if a court suit is brought we will have to fight it and you must understand that it will not be a token fight."

Faubus' jaw tightened. "Well," he exclaimed, getting up to leave the room, "I will get a court suit! A suit will be filed and the judge will order you to delay."

The next day a suit, brought in the name of Mrs. Clyde Thomason, recording secretary of the Mothers League of Little Rock Central High School, was filed in Chancery Court, seeking a temporary injunction against school integration.

The action was heard two days later before Chancellor Murray O. Reed, with Mrs. Thomason as the first witness before a crowded courtroom. Mrs. Thomason testified that persons whom she declined to identify even in confidence to the judge had told her "in strict confidence" that violence was "brewing" in connection with the opening of school the following Tuesday. She had heard "rumors that two gangs are forming, one of white boys and the other colored boys," and that one gang had guns and knives.

"The mothers are terrified," she concluded, "and are afraid to send their children to Central High School."

Police Chief Potts, Dr. Cooper and I also testified. Potts said he had found no evidence of planned violence and Dr. Cooper said none was expected. I explained preparations being made for school opening and said I had been assured the police would be ready to act if necessary, although no violence was anticipated. We made clear, however, we did not know what might be planned by persons from outside Little Rock.

But the main witness of the day was Governor Faubus himself, who had been subpoenaed by the plaintiff. As he walked into the tense courtroom, a young mother rushed up to him with her hands clasped and cried: "Governor, just see that there isn't any violence! We don't want our children mixed up in violence!"

Faubus testified that, to his personal knowledge, revolvers had been taken from both white and Negro students, but he did not elaborate. He said that until a month previous he had believed that Little Rock residents, while opposed to desegregation, were prepared to respect the Supreme Court's order. But, he continued, there had been a change recently, particularly since the visit of Governor Griffin, and he was now of the opinion that it was the worst possible time to start school integration. He noted that spokesmen for the segregationists disavowed violence, but that "a crowd can assemble with the best intentions and become a mob just because of two or three hot-headed people." This, he said, was not a matter that could be safely left in the hands of school officials.

In this way, the Governor seemed to be putting himself on the side of the White Citizens' Council and, as the *Arkansas Gazette* said editorially, he "abjectly surrendered when it was no longer possible to continue straddling the major issue."

Attorney House, for the School Board, argued that a mere allegation that bloodshed will occur did not make it so, but Attorney Griffin Smith, representing Mrs. Thomason, insisted there was a question as to whether local authorities could handle the situation if violence erupted. "There is fear of many persons sending children to school that violence may erupt," he said. "It has happened in a number of communities. We don't want to take the chance that it will happen here."

In his ruling, Judge Reed put special emphasis on testimony regarding the threat of violence and the opinion of the Governor. "I feel," he concluded, "that I can only rule to grant the injunction against starting integration."

The ruling left the School Board dangling between conflicting federal and state court orders and House, at the request of the Board, went immediately to the federal district court to ask for relief. For some time, there had been a vacancy in the federal judgeship for the eastern district of Arkansas. But a few days earlier, Judge Ronald N. Davies of North Dakota had arrived on temporary assignment to the post, and the Little Rock integration case was assigned to him. Judge Davies agreed to hear the School Board's plea the next day, August 30.

II

In this period, agitators were becoming more and more active in Little Rock and various anonymous threats were telephoned or written to School Board members and to me. Some were obviously from harmless crackpots, but I reported them to the police and once mentioned them to Faubus, who remarked that he was familiar with that kind of thing and they were always just threats.

Then, on the eve of the hearing before Judge Davies, the elder of my two daughters received a call from an unidentified man.

"You girls will not be alive this time tomorrow," he said, and hung up. As a result of such threats, the police and the School Board advised me to send my family away, and they did go to another town to visit relatives for a few days.

On Friday, four days before school opened, Judge Davies listened to arguments of attorneys for both sides and then nullified the temporary injunction granted by the state court to Mrs. Thomason, ordered the Board to proceed with integration on the following Tuesday and issued an injunction of his own restraining all persons from interfering.

That evening the School Board once more attempted to enlist the aid of the Governor, who met with us at a hotel. Governor Luther Hodges of North Carolina had just issued a firm warning that he would not tolerate violence in connection with school integration in that state, and we hoped Faubus would follow his example.

"We are concerned only about possible violence from the outside," R. A. Lile, a member of the Board, told the Governor. "We don't know whether we could get the help of the National Guard if it is needed. But if you will issue a statement like the Hodges statement we won't need the National Guard."

"If I make such a statement," Faubus replied, "it would make me look like an integrationist."

"Well, issue the statement," Secretary Upton suggested, "but add that you will use any legal means under the state segregation laws to oppose integration. That will make your position clear."

Faubus was angry, almost belligerent, as he rose to leave. "I don't know what I'll do," he exclaimed, looking at me, "but when I decide I'll tell Virgil."

I was not hopeful. I felt that the segregationist pressure on

Faubus had now become almost intolerable and developments the next day seemed to confirm this. I must go back a little to explain what happened. At one time when the Governor had expressed concern about "what the federals are going to do," I had said to him: "Why don't you ask them?"

"Whom would you talk to?" he asked.

"Well," I replied, "the Attorney General is Herbert Brownell."

Faubus did get in touch with the Department of Justice and late in August a former Arkansan, Arthur B. Caldwell, assistant to the Assistant Attorney General in Washington, arrived in Little Rock and discussed all phases of the integration problem with me. He didn't give me any idea what, if anything, the "federals" were going to do but he said he would talk with Faubus and others. And he asked that his visit be kept a close secret.

I heard nothing more about Caldwell's efforts until the day after Judge Davies' order to proceed—Saturday—when big headlines in the local newspaper said it had been disclosed in Washington that Faubus had conferred with the Department of Justice representative. The disclosure did the Governor no good politically and his quick, angry reaction to Washington's "betrayal" of a confidence indicated the intense pressure to which he was being subjected.

"I wanted to know," he told local reporters bitterly, "what, if anything, could be expected from the federal government in the way of assistance if disorders occur. This man [Caldwell] talked about court procedures and ended by saying there was virtually nothing they could do to help except issue court decrees."

He added that the federal government was trying to "make an object lesson" out of Arkansas and "use us to breach the South" on integration. But, he added, the Department of Justice had broken the agreement to keep the Caldwell talks confidential and "now you can see how much faith you can put in the national administration." As for the School Board's integration plan, he said nobody had asked him for help, and added: "I know the people don't want it."

I might mention here that I learned later that Faubus indirectly had been in touch with another branch of the government in regard to integration. A person close to Faubus telephoned an influential member of Congress—not from Arkansas—and talked about the possibility of action by the Governor to prevent enforcement of the Supreme Court's order. Then he asked: "If the Governor acts and the federals try to do something about it, can you keep him out of jail?"

The School Board was meeting every day now in preparation for the opening of school, and on Saturday it issued a formal statement saying that in view of the federal court orders it was "compelled to proceed with the first phase of desegregation of the schools. We earnestly solicit and confidently expect the understanding and co-operation of all students and adults in the peaceful solution of this problem."

Both Little Rock daily newspapers published editorials urging co-operation. The *Arkansas Democrat* said:

> The Little Rock School Board has a right to the community support it asked Sunday. . . . It has handled the integration question with rare diplomacy and skill . . . it worked out a plan that gives the least possible integration in the longest possible period of time. . . . Superintendent Blossom gave us leadership, calm and wise, which earns the fullest public backing. . . . A deplorable note in the situation was Governor Faubus' talk last week of possible disorder, and the inability of the federal government to stop it. Has he so little confidence in the good sense of our people? . . . Few Little Rockians want integration, but it's the verdict of the courts. And most of us know that all of life is a compromise. . . . And the integration compromise in our schools is an exceptionally favorable one, thanks to Superintendent Blossom and the School Board.

The *Arkansas Gazette* said:

> We do not believe any organized group of citizens would under any circumstances undertake to do violence to school children of any race. And if there are any individuals who might embark upon such a

reckless and indefensible course we have no doubt that our law enforcement officers can and will preserve order. This is a time of testing for all of us. Few of us are entirely happy over the necessary developments. . . . But certainly we must recognize that the School Board is simply carrying out its clear duty—and is doing so in the ultimate best interests of all the school children of Little Rock, white and colored alike. We are confident that the citizens of Little Rock will demonstrate . . . for the world to see that we are a law-abiding people.

Late Saturday, Lile and I were talking about whether it might still be possible to influence Faubus to make a public statement and we agreed that it would be wise to ask Winthrop Rockefeller, whom Faubus had made head of the Arkansas Industrial Development Commission, to talk to the Governor. We telephoned Rockefeller and then drove sixty-five miles to his mountaintop farm, Winrock, to discuss our idea. Rockefeller felt that a peaceful solution of the integration problem was important to the work of the AIDC and he arranged to confer with Faubus Sunday afternoon. After their talk, Lile and I met him at a hotel. He said: "I don't think I got very far, and I don't know what he's going to do."

Discouraged, I went home and was in bed around 10 P.M. but the telephone awakened me half an hour later. It was the Governor, asking me whether I could come to the mansion immediately. I said I could and I got dressed and drove over.

Faubus was waiting for me in a large den in one wing of the big mansion. My first thought as I entered was that he looked very tired. His expression was serious, his dark eyes brooding. He asked me to sit down and then he dropped down on a big divan. The night was hot and he had his coat off and the collar of his white shirt was open. He asked an aide to bring iced tea and drank it thirstily and then leaned back on the divan, putting his feet up on a coffee table.

We talked for about three hours, for the most part reviewing things we had discussed in earlier conversations. I think perhaps I did most of the talking, and at times the Governor seemed to be sunk in serious meditation. He was pleasant and understanding, and there were several times when I was almost convinced that he was going to agree to issue the statement requested by the School Board. I felt that he wanted to go along with us. But he was still vague.

His personal belief, he said, was that we could integrate the senior high school on Tuesday with only minor incidents. He agreed that there was no prospect of violence unless it came from the outside, and he considered that unlikely.

"Governor," I said, "we have worked almost three years to get past this problem peacefully. We will now succeed if only you will issue a statement that you will not tolerate defiance of the law."

He shook his head. "I'll call you," he said, "when I decide. . . . But I don't think I'm going to let you do it"—presumably meaning integrate.

III

At this point, just prior to opening of the Little Rock schools, it may be of interest to survey the progress—or the lack of it— that had been made in border and Southern states since the Supreme Court issued its school integration order in 1954. The following information was taken from an Associated Press dispatch, and reflected the situation at the end of the 1957 spring term.

Latest figures show there are now 674 school districts in Southern or border states where desegregation is either under way or completed, leaving about 3,000 still segregated.

At first glance, the figures appear to indicate marked progress in the last three years, with more than one-sixth of the 3,674 districts reported striving, with varied degrees of intensity, to obey the high tribunal's mandate. But the other five-sixths unquestionably represent a much tougher nut to crack.

Here, in brief, is a rundown on key states in the controversy, with indications as to the degree of progress toward desegregation in each and the state's official attitude.

Alabama—No progress; pro-segregation.

Delaware—Considerable progress; pro-integration at state level, generally leaning toward segregation at local level. About 22,751 whites and Negroes are attending integrated schools out of the state's total school enrollment of 63,954.

District of Columbia—Complete integration. White student enrollment dropped by 4,011 between October 1955 and October 1956, while Negro enrollment jumped 4,846. Steady white exodus to the suburbs may account for part of the drop in white enrollment. Negroes account for 63 per cent of district's total school enrollment.

Florida—No progress; moderate to strong pro-segregation.

Georgia—No progress; strongly pro-segregation.

Kentucky—Considerable progress; pro-integration. Public has generally accepted desegregation, but outbreaks of mob action in Clay and Sturgis brought out National Guard. Louisville has desegregated its schools. Weaverton and Henderson schools were boycotted in protest against desegregation.

Louisiana—No progress at elementary or secondary levels of public schools, but parochial (Catholic) schools have announced they will desegregate gradually. Official state attitude is strongly pro-segregation. Four of seven state-supported colleges have accepted Negroes as a result of court action. Four of nine private colleges accept Negroes.

Maryland—Considerable progress; strongly pro-integration. Thirteen of the state's 23 school districts plus Baltimore city have desegregated in practice but not all schools are mixed. More than one-fourth of students are Negroes.

Mississippi—No progress—strongly pro-segregation.

Missouri—Considerable progress; pro-integration. Only four high schools remain segregated. All 15 state-supported colleges now admit Negroes.

North Carolina—No progress except at college level; pro-segregation.

Oklahoma—Considerable progress; generally pro-integration. Out of 261 school districts having Negroes, 195 have begun to integrate. All 18 state-supported colleges accept Negroes.

South Carolina—No progress; strongly pro-segregation.

Tennessee—Slight progress; official attitude is neutral. About 8,870 whites and 261 Negroes are in "integrated situations" out of total of 627,781 whites and 128,165 Negro students. Clinton high school, scene of racial violence, is only desegregated school in the state. Nashville has announced plans to desegregate.

Texas—Some progress; official attitude is divided. Out of 1,802 school districts 104 have begun to desegregate. Of 46 formerly all-white colleges, 19 now accept Negroes.

Virginia—No progress at primary and secondary school levels; official attitude is "massive resistance" against desegregation.

West Virginia—Considerable progress; pro-integration. Only three school districts in the state remain segregated.

The school integration progress in Arkansas was, in some ways, more advanced than in other Southern states, and it was interesting that Governor Faubus' past record had favored integration in various categories. As he pointed out in an address, all transportation systems had been integrated under his administration and six of the seven state colleges had Negro students. (In Little Rock, hospitals, libraries and certain other public facilities were integrated.) He was the first Democratic governor in the South to put Negroes on a Democratic state committee and he recommended to the Democratic state convention that the so-called "white primary" be abolished. During his administration, Negroes had been appointed to administrative positions never before held by members of their race. His son attended a state-supported integrated college, and eight public schools in other Arkansas towns had been "peaceably integrated" during his tenure in office.

A survey of school integration in Arkansas early in September of 1957, by the *Arkansas Democrat*, showed the following:

Integration began in Arkansas on a frosty morning in February, 1948. Silas Hunt, a 25-year-old combat veteran of World War II and a Negro, enrolled in the University of Arkansas Law School. . . .

On May 21, 1954, the Fayetteville school board decided to admit five Negroes to its previously all white school. . . .

These events marked the first time that a Negro had attended a white college or a high school in any of the 11 states that make up what is known as the "solid South" or the "Confederacy."

Today, with the single exception of Texas, Arkansas is far ahead of any of them in its record of compliance.

The record to date: The state has eight school districts that have at least one class attended by both Negro and white students. And six out of seven state-supported colleges have now or have had Negro students.

Also remarkable is the fact that integration has come about voluntarily in all but one of these cases. . . .

Based on information from various sources, about 86 Negroes have begun classes with white pupils in eight cities. The range is from one in Ft. Smith to 23 in Van Buren. Enrollment is not complete at some colleges and most of them report that they do not differentiate in registration procedures for Negroes or whites which were the reasons given by college officials for vague announcements as to numbers. But probably, based on attendance in past years there will be about 33 Negroes enrolled at six out of the seven state-supported schools. . . .

IV

On Monday, September 2, the newspapers were filled with articles and comments on the opening of school the next day. There were reports on sermons that had been preached on both sides of the integration issue. Segregationist leaders, sensing success, sent Faubus telegrams of encouragement. The United States Attorney's office issued a statement that the full resources of the Department of Justice, including the Federal Bureau of Investigation and U.S. marshals, stood ready to investigate any complaints of interference with federal court orders. Faubus told reporters he had heard new reports of possible violence but said that rumors he would declare martial law were "strictly rumors." A former chief justice of the state supreme court said in a Labor Day speech at Prairie Grove that "unless cool heads prevail there is danger of bloodshed" at Little Rock.

Tension was so high that eight of the seventeen Negro students who had enrolled and been approved to attend Central High School came to my office and withdrew. Nine others and some two thousand white children prepared to start the school term on Tuesday.

At noon on Monday I talked with Police Chief Potts and he asked me to find out from the Governor whether he would make the National Guard available if it was needed and, if so, whom the police should call in an emergency. I was unable to reach the Governor immediately by telephone and then I was tied up in my office until about 2:30 P.M. At that time, my secretary, Mrs. Marguerite Warr, came, pale and shaken, to tell me that an anonymous telephone call had just been received. The caller said several extremist segregation leaders from other parts of the state had arrived or would soon arrive in Little Rock with more than 150 others who were "out to get Blossom."

In my office was Fred Graham, my assistant superintendent, who asked: "Shall I lock the front door?"

"No," I said. "Call the police and ask them to investigate."

I again tried to call the Governor but was not able to get him until after the police had arrived and Lieutenant Carl Jackson was sitting beside my desk. I told Faubus that the Police Chief wanted to know if the National Guard would be available in an emergency and whom he should call if he needed help. I also mentioned the anonymous warning I had received, and asked him where I could get in touch with the director of State Police in an emergency.

"Do you need protection?" the Governor asked.

"I don't know whether I do or not," I said. "Lieutenant Jackson is sitting here beside me."

"Do you need protection?" he repeated.

"Do you think I need protection?" I asked him.

"I wish you would write me a letter asking for it," he said.

"You know I won't do that," I replied and hung up the telephone. Turning to Jackson, I said: "I think Governor Faubus himself is behind this program of intimidation." Then I realized that the Governor had not answered any of the questions I had asked him.

Late that afternoon officers of the Police Department met with the School Board for a final check of plans. They told us they had not been able to find any signs of impending trouble, and believed the telephone warning to me was without foundation.

Although I didn't know it at the time, an announcement was made at the capitol that Faubus would speak that night over radio and television. This immediately started rumors that he would call out the National Guard, but the Governor's office refused to make any announcements.

"The Governor hasn't even started writing his speech," one of his administrative assistants told reporters. He added that the text would be given to reporters as soon as the speech was written. A couple of hours later another aide said that no one but Faubus had any idea of what he would say in the speech, but that it would be "nothing of major importance."

Then, about six o'clock, I was called out of the School Board meeting to take a telephone call from a newspaperman.

"Did you hear Faubus is calling out the Guard?" he asked.

"No."

"Well, he is. I'll let you know what happens."

Shortly afterward a member of my staff telephoned to say that the Guard was moving into positions around Central High School and that Faubus would make his television speech at ten-fifteen. The reporters still didn't have copies of his speech—in fact they didn't get them until the Governor started speaking—and nobody could be sure of Faubus' purpose in calling out the guardsmen.

I informed the Board and upon checking we found that the National Guard had reached the school grounds about eight-thirty. It was then almost time for the Governor's speech, which we assumed would make his purpose clear, and we tuned a television set in to hear what he had to say.

Chapter Six

REGIMENTED

CONFUSION

GOVERNOR FAUBUS' SPEECH announcing that he had summoned the National Guard to surround Central High School was designed to establish a legal basis for thwarting integration, but he insisted that he was not defying the orders of the United States Supreme Court, nor even opposing desegregation.

He declared that the guardsmen would not act as segregationists or integrationists. He tried to establish that he was within his constitutional rights because he was acting only to preserve the peace and was not trying to circumvent the federal law—for which he might be subject to prosecution—by resorting to a subterfuge to prevent integration.

Since the previous Friday, he said, "evidence of discord, anger and resentment has come from so many sources as to become a deluge." He said that I had appealed to him for help, presumably an inaccurate version of my conversation asking him whether the National Guard would be available in an emergency. He referred to a telephone campaign "of massive proportions" that was under-

73

way to get mothers of white children to assemble at the high
school early Tuesday for demonstrations. He reported that "cara-
vans" of persons from other parts of the state were moving
"peaceably" on the city and that there had been an unusually
large sale of weapons in the Little Rock area—two statements that
were later shown to be inaccurate. Finally, he argued for a delay
on the grounds that litigation over validity of the state segregation
laws had not been concluded.

"We are faced . . . with forcible integration of public schools
against the overwhelming sentiment of the people of the area,"
he continued. "The . . . attempt will bring about widespread
disorder and violence. . . . I have therefore taken the following
action:

"Units of the National Guard have been, or are now being
mobilized with the mission to maintain or restore the peace and
good order of this community. Advance units are already on duty
on the grounds of Central High School. . . .

"This is a decision I have reached prayerfully. It has been made
after conferences with dozens of people and after the checking
and verification of as many of the reports as possible.

"The mission of the State Militia is to maintain or restore
order and to protect the lives and property of citizens. They will
act not as segregationists or integrationists, but as soldiers called
to active duty to carry out their assigned tasks.

"But, I must state here in all sincerity, that it is my opinion—
yes, even a conviction, that it will not be possible to restore
or to maintain order and protect the lives and property of the
citizens if forcible integration is carried out tomorrow in the
schools of this community. The inevitable conclusion therefore,
must be that the schools in Pulaski County, for the time being,
must be operated on the same basis as they have been operated
in the past.

"I appeal now for reason, clear thinking and good order. Let
us all be good citizens, and continue as a people and a state, upon

the road of progress on which we have so enthusiastically embarked.
"The Public Peace Will Be Preserved."

When the Governor had finished, his position was still somewhat muddled. He had said the guardsmen would not take sides,
but that the schools must continue on a segregated basis. The
School Board went back into session and decided that, although
it was still under federal court orders to proceed with integration,
it would be a mistake to attempt to introduce Negroes into Central
High School the next morning. Later the following statement was
issued:

"Although the federal court has ordered integration to proceed,
Governor Faubus has said that schools should continue as they
have in the past and has stationed troops at Central High School
to maintain order. In view of this situation, we ask that no Negro
students attend Central or any other white high school until this
dilemma is legally resolved."

The statement was signed by all members of the Board: Dr.
Cooper; Harold J. Engstrom, Jr., vice president; Wayne Upton,
secretary; Dr. Dale Alford, R. A. Lile and Henry V. Rath.

At the same time, the North Little Rock School Board, which
had been scheduled to start integration of seven high school seniors
the following Monday voted unanimously to delay action "until
the status of the problem of integration has been fully cleared
by the Courts." To this formal statement, a member of the Board
added: "We don't want the National Guard camped on our door-
step."

After the Little Rock Board meeting ended, I collected members of my staff and discussed plans for the next day. This brought
up the question of how students would identify themselves to the
guardsmen and who would be permitted to enter the school. I
telephoned Brigadier General Sherman T. Clinger, head of the
Arkansas National Guard, and he later came to my office to work
out the details.

"Will people entering the school need some kind of special identification?" I asked.

"Well," Clinger replied, "no Negroes will be permitted to enter."

"Does that include janitors and cooks and other staff personnel?"

"Yes," he said. "Those are orders from my chief and I intend to carry them out."

I began to feel that Faubus' real purpose was to force closure of the school. His orders, of course, completely disrupted the school routine, particularly in connection with serving lunch to some two thousand students the next day. My staff and I worked all night rounding up volunteers, shifting personnel from other schools and doing whatever we could to meet the emergency. The order to bar Negro staff personnel was soon rescinded, but for the next four days or so I never did get to bed, and my staff got little sleep.

Early on Tuesday morning—probably about two o'clock—I inspected the building and grounds at Central High School, where General Clinger had taken over the principal's office as headquarters. I talked to some of the soldiers and officers. One officer was an old friend of mine.

"When did you find out about the Guard being called?" he asked me.

"Last night," I replied. "About six o'clock."

He laughed. "I got orders last Friday," he said, "that the Guard was being mobilized."

When, at dawn, I saw several hundred soldiers standing almost shoulder to shoulder around Central High School I could feel only a deep sadness. My life had been devoted to public education in the state of Arkansas. For almost thirty years, I had seen as part of my everyday experience the improvement of teaching standards, the progress in methods of education, in housing of students and in equipment at their disposal. I had watched class after class arrive as chattering, wide-eyed youngsters. I had seen them grow up to be young men and women with, I fervently hoped,

a purpose in life and an ability to achieve it. We had faced big
and difficult obstacles in the Arkansas educational system, but we
had gone forward, too; and I hoped I had done all that I could
to help. My career, my whole interest, were bound up in that
hope of future progress.

There was, to be sure, still a long way to go, and on that Tuesday morning the road ahead looked longer and harder than ever.
Now there might be no way to avoid a showdown with bigotry
and racial prejudice. The work of many years might be destroyed
in a moment of blind emotional rebellion against the democratic
process of law and order. I felt that, under the pressure and
propaganda and threats and flattery of extremist leaders, Faubus
had struck a blow that would do more than anything else to
convince the people they did not have to obey this particular law.
And that, I believed, could only do great injury to our young people
—not to mention damage to our system of public education.

Later, I discussed these thoughts with various public leaders,
and one of the most influential Southern Congressmen told me
I had underestimated the damage done that night.

"When Faubus called out the National Guard," he said, "he
did the South a great disservice. Prior to that, Southern politicians
could hide behind the Court's orders, but Faubus slammed the
door on moderation and on any compromise solution. Afterward,
few Southern governors would dare take any less adamant stand
because of the political consequences, although some might have
desired and been able to do so if Faubus had not established the
pattern."

II

The next morning about five hundred white teen-agers and adults
gathered outside Central High School as students returned to
classes after the summer vacation. No Negroes appeared. As the
morning went on, an air of defiance and triumph spread among

the crowd. The power of the state was on the side of the mob.

That morning—Tuesday—Governor Faubus told reporters that he had been deluged with calls and telegrams saying he had "saved the state." The National Guard would remain at the school as long as there remained a possibility of violence, he said. He insisted at that time that he had told the guardsmen only that their mission was to maintain peace and order, thus avoiding placing himself in contempt of the federal Court. The guardsmen, he said at one point, "may use their discretion about admitting Negroes." He also accused me of having told him one thing and the courts another in regard to the danger of violence at the school.

In an editorial entitled "The Crisis Mr. Faubus Made," the *Arkansas Gazette* said that

dozens of local reporters and national correspondents worked through the day [Tuesday] without verifying the few facts the Governor offered to explain why his appraisal of the danger of violence was so different from that of local officials. . . . Now it remains for Mr. Faubus to decide whether he intends to pose what could be the most serious constitutional question to face the national government since the Civil War. The effect of his action so far is to interpose his state office between the local School District and the United States Court. . . . Thus the issue is no longer segregation vs. integration. The question has now become the supremacy of the government of the United States in all matters of law. . . . If Mr. Faubus, in fact, has no intention of defying federal authority now is the time for him to call a halt to the resistance which is preventing the carrying out of a duly entered court order. And certainly he should do so before his own actions become the cause of the violence he professes to fear.

The School Board, again caught in the middle, decided that it had no choice but to return to Judge Davies. Attorney House appeared before the Judge after filing a petition that the Board should not be held in contempt of the Court. He explained that the stationing of troops at the school had prompted the Board to ask Negro students to remain away solely for their own safety. He

asked the Judge for instructions as to whether the request addressed
to the Negro students should be rescinded.

"The School Board will do whatever you say is fitting and proper
under the circumstances," he added.

Judge Davies said he had read Faubus' speech and noted that the
soldiers were at the school only to maintain order, and were neither
integrationists nor segregationists. "I am taking these statements
of the Governor at full face value," he said. He then ordered the
Board to "put into effect forthwith" its plan of integration.

That evening the School Board issued a statement that Central
High School would be open to Negro students the next morning.

Davies also ordered that the FBI, under direction of the United
States Attorney, Orso Cobb, "begin at once a full, thorough and
complete investigation" into responsibility for interference with the
Court's integration order.

Meantime, the Mothers League renewed its telephone campaign
to get mothers of white students to gather for demonstrations the
next morning outside the school. Segregationists also began circulating petitions asking that I be fired as Superintendent of Schools.

Late that evening, when a reporter asked the Governor whether
Judge Davies' order to proceed with integration would affect the
actions of the National Guard, Faubus replied that he didn't
know whether or not the guardsmen would be ordered to admit
Negro students on Wednesday.

III

On Wednesday morning at about eight o'clock, a slight, dusky
girl wearing sunglasses and a freshly-ironed white dress and carrying school books under her arm approached the intersection of
Fourteenth Street and Park Avenue, adjacent to Central High
School. At the corner, Arkansas National Guardsmen wearing
helmets and carrying rifles drew together, forming a solid line

that blocked the girl's progress. The soldiers stared straight ahead and said nothing.

Looking neither to the right nor left, the girl turned and crossed to the opposite side of the street in front of the school building. She walked a few steps and then recrossed toward the main school entrance. Again, guardsmen lining the sidewalk pressed closely together to block her path. She swerved and walked steadily down the line of troops seeking an opening to the school grounds. She found none.

Suddenly, as the newspapers reported it later, about two hundred white adults further down the street saw her, and broke into a run to interrupt her line of march, shouting:

"Don't let her in our school—that nigger!"

"Why don't you go to your own school?"

A woman lunged at the girl, crying: "Go back where you came from!" but a guardsman pushed her back.

Trembling, but never losing her dignity, the Negro girl made a third vain effort to walk through the line of soldiers. Then she went back across the street and sat down on a bus stop bench at the corner. Tears were in her eyes. Some of the crowd followed, shouting abuse. A newspaper reporter learned only that her name was Elizabeth Eckford, that she was fifteen years old and legally enrolled in Central High School. A white woman who spoke to her kindly was jeered by the crowd. A bus came along and the girl climbed aboard.

That short but highly emotional scene on the fourth day of September, 1957, was one that Little Rock would not soon forget. Photographers recorded it, almost step by step, and one photograph of a white girl screaming imprecations at Elizabeth Eckford was spread across front pages of newspapers throughout the country and abroad. It was later republished as an advertisement—I don't know who paid for it—in a Little Rock newspaper, with a short caption: "God help us all!"

Elizabeth Eckford's experience set the pattern for that first, futile day of "integration." The second Negro student to appear was Terrance Roberts, also fifteen, and the son of a kitchen worker at the North Little Rock Veterans Hospital. He, too, was turned back by the guardsmen. Later the other seven students arrived at the school accompanied by several adult Negroes, including Harry Bass, a Negro leader in Little Rock. The guardsmen motioned them away and they stepped into the street, where they were met by Lieutenant Colonel Marion Johnson, commanding the troops. Bass asked if the soldiers were preventing them from entering the school and Johnson replied in the affirmative.

"I just want to get this straight," Bass then said. "You are doing this on the orders of the Governor—is that correct?"

"That is right," Johnson replied.

The Negroes departed. There had been no serious demonstrations during these episodes although there were jeers and shouts and a few young spectators had attempted to lunge at the Negroes, only to be seized by the soldiers, searched for weapons and then thrust back into the crowd. A few boys wearing Confederate caps waved a Confederate flag and another group, including Mrs. Thomason, the woman who had brought suit to halt integration, loudly sang "Dixie." No effort was made to disperse the demonstrators and, as the hours passed, the segregationists became jubilant because they realized nobody was going to interfere with them unless they committed acts of violence. Conditions were ideal for rule by the mob.

There were some interesting comments later on the day's events by Elizabeth Eckford and Terrance Roberts, as quoted by the Associated Press:

Terrance said that he had received one telephone call a few hours after he tried to enter all-white Little Rock Central and was turned back by armed National Guardsmen.

He said that the caller, who sounded like a young white girl, told him: "Don't come back to Central tomorrow; go to Horace Mann." (Negro High School)

The jeers that came from the segregationists in the crowd that gathered at Little Rock Central apparently were a surprise to both Terrance and Elizabeth Eckford.

Both said that they did not expect any trouble as far as violence or threats are concerned.

"I didn't think it would go this far," Terrance said, referring to the boos and insults that came from the crowd. He said he had expected to enter the school up until the time he actually stood face-to-face with a silent Guardsman who blocked his way.

Why did he try to enter the white school? Prompting, perhaps from the National Association for the Advancement of Colored People?

"Nobody urged me to go," he said. "The school board asked if I wanted to go. I thought if I got in some of the other kids would be able to get in . . . and have more opportunities." In answer to a question, he said his parents are not members of the NAACP.

Both Terrance and Elizabeth feel that Central is a better school than Horace Mann, and Elizabeth advanced a definite argument.

"I want to be a lawyer," said the shy, slightly-built girl. "I want to go to Central so that I can take speech. There's no speech course at Horace Mann."

Was she scared when she walked the two blocks in front of Little Rock Central with hundreds of people around her almost all the way?

"Whoooo, yes," she said with a grin.

Both Terrance and Elizabeth believe that there will be "embarrassing social problems" if they attend Central, but they do not believe them to be insurmountable.

The Eckfords have five other children. Oscar Eckford works for a railroad and Mrs. Eckford teaches blind and deaf Negro students "how to wash and iron for themselves."

"I have sixty students," she says proudly.

Does Mrs. Eckford believe that there will be awkward social situations if there is integration?

"See that vacant lot across the street," she said. "Negro and white children play ball there and they get along fine."

Other comments in the newspapers by white students included these:

Boy—"Why don't they let the kids handle this situation? If the Negroes had come in the first day, all there would have been were a few whistles and catcalls."

Boy—"I think Faubus prevented a lot of potential trouble . . . [but] it wouldn't be long before the trouble settled down. You can't fight the federal court."

Boy—"I am against integration at present. I think there will be violence if some older people keep egging the situation on. I think Faubus did the right thing."

Girl—"Faubus made a big fool of himself. I feel sorry for those nine Negroes."

Girl—"If the parents left everything alone, everything would be okay."

Girl—"There is no reason for Negroes to come to our school. If they do, there will be violence."

I was also interested in an article published a few days later by Miss Elizabeth Burrow, part owner of *The Ozark Spectator*. Miss Burrow was recuperating from an operation for cancer, but she had lost none of her well-known sparkle when she sat down to write a piece about a similar school integration controversy in her own town:

All too frequently white people have black hearts. I first learned that in school here in Ozark, where a few town kids used to pick on the country kids.

That was all so long ago, I thought everybody would be different by now. Just as we have a superior class of Negroes here, so I'd thought that our white citizens were extra special, too.

Most of them are, thank God.

Certainly our Negro population is too small ever to present a problem, and our integration is not noble. It's simply horse-sense. . . .

Of course, the [Negro children] will make it all right. But the worry is over our own conscience. Will we white people make it all right?

Here's a malignancy worse than my cancer, and I wouldn't swap with you.

Not very many persons in Little Rock were speaking out as frankly as Miss Burrow at the end of the first day on which Negro students were turned back from Central High School. Despite all that had happened, Governor Faubus continued to insist that he was using the National Guard only to preserve the peace. But if anybody had any doubt as to his true purpose, it was resolved when a reporter overheard a National Guard officer talking to one of his soldiers at the high school.

"Do you know what your orders are?" the officer asked.

"Yes, sir," the soldier answered briskly. "Keep the niggers out!"

Chapter Seven

WHO'S IN CHARGE?

THE TRIUMPH of mob rule, abetted by the Arkansas National Guard under orders of Governor Faubus, not only prevented integration of Negroes into Little Rock Central High School at the opening of the 1957-58 term, but turned the first week of classes into nightmare for students and faculty.

Noisy crowds of adult segregationists—often numbering several hundred—gathered daily outside the school to demonstrate in support of Faubus and to make certain that nine enrolled Negro students did not renew their attempt to pass through the lines of guardsmen around the building. Sometimes the demonstrators milled about furiously, shouting at each other or at children who could be seen at classroom windows. Again they broke into song —usually "Dixie"—and waved Confederate flags as a symbol of their defiance of the school integration orders of the United States Supreme Court.

National Guard officers occasionally ordered them to cease such demonstrations but with no more than momentary success. If they imposed silence on one group of rowdy demonstrators, another group further down the street would immediately break into shouts and song. The noise went on—and nothing at all was

85

done about forcing the idle crowds to disperse. As a result, the atmosphere of hysteria mounted, the worst possible example of adult citizenship was presented daily to students at Central High School and there was so much confusion that it became impossible to provide an atmosphere conducive to proper education.

Later, looking back on the weeks of late August and early September, it would not be easy for anyone to explain exactly how or why the change came about. Little Rock's newspapers had stood firmly for respect for the law, the city officials and civic leaders had worked for a peaceful solution, the people generally had accepted the idea of minimum school integration—in fact, Little Rock was probably the least segregated in all categories of any border state city.

Yet one main reason for the Little Rock crisis was obvious. When the Supreme Court delivered its judgment and the time came to act on a problem of great national concern, the federal government had no plan and no policy for carrying out the law, or even for assisting the Little Rock School Board in its efforts to obey it. The FBI's reinforced staff investigated and investigated but the Department of Justice did nothing constructive—and even two years later had done little except complain that it was hamstrung by weak provisions for enforcement of civil rights laws. Even after the situation at Central High School had become so chaotic as to threaten destruction of the public school system the federal government provided no leadership and no planned action that could lead to a solution or even to enforcement of the Court's orders except by the military.

I do not want to leave the impression that I was the only one who was aware of the lack of preparedness in Washington in the early days of September. It was general knowledge, as was illustrated by a dispatch from the capital by Lyle C. Wilson, the veteran manager of the United Press in Washington:

The Eisenhower administration was not ready for the Little Rock school integration emergency.

The president left for a Rhode Island vacation. White House staff chief Sherman Adams is off to a New Hampshire speaking engagement. Democrats will be asking: Who was keeping the store?

Attorney General Herbert Brownell Jr. was on the job but without any immediate strategy or policy to pursue. The battle of headlines had been favoring Arkansas' Governor Faubus, who doubtless planned it that way.

There has been a feeling around town that Brownell was stalling for time or a policy inspiration. . . .

This Arkansas dispute is not directly connected with the Eisenhower civil rights bill recently limited by Congress to voting rights. The president has not yet signed that bill, although he is expected to do so shortly.

Even so, Mr. Eisenhower probably is in an easier position today with respect to Arkansas developments than he would have been if Congress had passed his civil rights bill as he proposed it. Before the Senate began rejecting major portions of that legislation, the language very definitely committed the president to use federal troops in support of any civil right whatsoever. . . .

II

The future could not be clearly foreseen during the opening week of school in 1957, but after only a few days the confusion had become so great and the possibility of getting Negro students into the school had become so slight that some drastic action had to be taken. On Thursday, the School Board decided it had no choice but to apply to Federal Judge Ronald N. Davies for a temporary delay in starting integration. At the time, race rioting seemed imminent and the Board's action was encouraged by the United States District Attorney.

The Board's petition said that tension was developing inside the school, that parents were forming antagonistic groups, that education was impossible and that the court was requested temporarily to stay its order for integration until calm could be restored to a point where intelligence could be substituted for emotional agitation "for the good of all pupils."

Two days later, Davies heard arguments on the petition in a crowded courtroom. No sooner had the attorneys concluded than he picked up a sheet of paper from his desk and began reading his decision, creating the impression—rightly or wrongly—that it had been written even before he came into court to hear the arguments. "There can be nothing but chaos if court decrees are flouted," he said in announcing that he was refusing any delay.

"What did the testimony this morning disclose? Beyond the bald and unsupported statements in the petition, only the testimony of the Little Rock superintendent of schools was offered, and that bore upon the desirability of the proper education of children in the Little Rock schools with which sentiments we must all agree.

"The testimony and arguments this morning were, in my judgment, as anemic as the petition itself; and the position taken by the school directors does violence to my concept of the duty of the petitioners to adhere with resolution to its own approved plan of gradual integration in the Little Rock public schools.

"It must never be thought that this court has not given careful consideration to this problem and all that it entails, but it must never be forgotten that I have a constitutional duty and obligation from which I shall not shrink. This court is not persuaded that upon the tenuous showing made by the petitioners this morning that it should suspend enforcement of the petitioners' plan of integration."

The decision put the School Board and me right back on the same old merry-go-round, under orders to integrate but with no power to do it. Actually, our outlook was more hopeless than ever because segregationists were quick to claim that the Judge had made up his mind even before he heard the arguments and was determined to ram integration through at any cost. The abruptness of the decision also angered many moderate friends of the Board.

The Board itself now felt that all hands were raised against our honest and carefully prepared program for observing the Supreme Court decisions under very difficult circumstances. We had had no help from any branch of government. The segregationist minority had intimidated many persons who might have co-operated with us but remained as silent bystanders. And now the federal court had denounced us in a humiliating fashion. By failing to show any human understanding of our problem, the court had publicly slapped those who attempted to uphold the law while those who sought to overthrow the law were able to demonstrate and agitate freely. There had been a restraining injunction, general in nature, against any interference with school integration, but the crowds continued to gather, to carry segregationist placards and to demonstrate. On various occasions, I inquired whether information regarding the demonstrations had been forwarded to the Department of Justice and was told that the Department was being kept fully informed of developments. Yet nothing was done to stop the agitation. I began to feel that the School Board and I were about to touch bottom for the third time.

Governor Faubus was busy issuing a statement or two every day. He told reporters he had heard federal authorities were planning to take him into custody. He indicated belief that his telephone had been tapped by federal agents. He sought to create the impression he was in some kind of danger by having the Governor's mansion surrounded on all sides by National Guardsmen. He sent a telegram to President Eisenhower to the effect that the whole crisis had been caused by a federal judge who misunderstood "our problems." Then he sent another telegram to the President, apparently in an effort to show that he was not really defying the Supreme Court, offering to turn over his "evidence" that violence was imminent when he called out the troops and that the danger was still growing. He never did reveal any "evidence."

One of Faubus' telegrams insisted that the issue was not integration versus segregation and pointed out that integration had proceeded smoothly at the University and other schools.

"As governor of Arkansas," he added, "I appeal to you to use your good offices to modify the extreme stand and stop the unwarranted interference of federal agents in this area so that we may again enjoy the domestic tranquility and continue in our pursuit of ideal relations with the races. Time is the essence of the situation with which I am confronted."

The argument that he had acted legally and only to maintain public order had become the keystone of the Governor's official position. It was not a very solid keystone but it was one that the segregation extremists were eager to support by staging threatening gestures when necessary. Mayor Woodrow Mann of Little Rock, a moderate, attacked Faubus for staging "a political farce" to prevent school integration. He said there had not been "a shred of evidence" that justified calling out the troops but that he (Mann) was now receiving reports of "planned, manufactured racial incidents" that would be started by "rabble-rousers, who will try to give credence to Governor Faubus' stand."

That night the extremists made his words ring true by burning a big fiery cross on the Mayor's lawn.

III

The weekend of September 8 was tense, with Governor Faubus going on a national television network to criticize the federal court as high-handed and with dispatches from Washington predicting early action—details unspecified—by the Department of Justice.

In his television speech, Faubus said that "the price is too high and the danger too great" for him to permit integration to be forced on the school. "Maybe Negro leaders and white integrationist leaders and even Federal Judge Davies are willing to sacrifice the lives of a certain number of people in this community in order to take one more step toward final and complete integration of the schools," he continued. "Be that their philosophy. It is not mine."

He argued that the constitution did not say that the nine Negro students denied admittance to the school had to be allowed to attend at this time. The Supreme Court's order for "all deliberate speed," he said, meant that it recognized integration could be accomplished in some communities in days, in other communities in weeks and in other communities in months. Still other communities, he said, may require years for a period of transition.

"The constitution of the state of Arkansas and of the United States imposed upon me," he said, "the duty to maintain the public peace and to use the militia, if, in my judgment, it is necessary. I cannot abdicate my office and let a federal judge substitute his judgment for mine on this issue. If he has a right to substitute his judgment for mine on this issue, then he has the right to substitute his judgment on all issues involving duties imposed upon me as governor of Arkansas. If this be the law, then every state in this union is nothing more than a vassal state to a central government. This strikes at the very heart of our system of government composed of a dual sovereignty."

Meanwhile, Thurgood Marshall, chief counsel for the NAACP, had arrived from New York to consult on procedure with Wiley Branton, the organization's state attorney. Marshall not only expressed opposition to any delay in integration, but said that it might have been better if there had been complete integration at once.

"There's strength in numbers," he told a reporter, "especially where you're having trouble. One student [integrated in a white school] is horrible and nine or ten is bad. Maybe we ought to take all those who are eligible to attend integrated schools in Little Rock and see it out."

A group of sixteen ministers issued a statement condemning Faubus' action in the integration crisis and later his position was "deplored" by twenty-seven Methodist ministers attending a pastors' school at Conway, Arkansas, and by the Arkansas Christian

Missionary Society Board, an agency of the Christian churches of Arkansas.

Newspaper comment in the nation generally was concerned with the Governor's speech and his action in calling out the National Guard. A few examples follow:

Knoxville News-Sentinel—Little Rock was dealing rationally with a hard problem until the Governor intervened. Now he's caught with his foot in his mouth.

Birmingham Post-Herald—Despite his unquestionable authority to use the National Guard to preserve peace and maintain order, the mistake Governor Faubus made was to draw the line so sharply between state and federal authority as to demand a showdown.

Chattanooga News-Free Press—. . . The illegal aggressor is not the governor of Arkansas who seeks to maintain the status quo as desired by the majority of his people. The aggressor is a lawless Supreme Court bent on unconstitutional sociological reform.

Miami Herald—Only one outcome is possible. The supremacy of the federal government will prevail. It is unfortunate that the true substance of states' rights will be obscured and weakened by the fog of emotions stirred by developments at Little Rock.

Charlotte, (N.C.) Observer—President Eisenhower, a patient and forbearing man, cannot afford to let Faubus get away with it.

Anderson (S.C.) Independent—If blood is to be shed that blood will be upon the hands of Dwight D. Eisenhower and the anti-South party in power.

New York Herald Tribune—Wiser heads than that of Governor Faubus . . . know that every effort of responsible Southern senators during the recent civil rights debate was directed toward avoiding a head-on collision between foes and supporters of equal rights, toward averting the appeal to armed forces which the governor has invoked. Their only course now can be to endeavor to undo the damage Mr. Faubus has so recklessly wrought; to acknowledge that his tactics represent in themselves a lost cause, with no reason, dignity nor patriotism to gild its doom.

Detroit News—Governor Faubus has deliberately exaggerated the tensions and put together ingredients for a political crisis which could and should have been avoided. If he is right, then the law of the land is not all the Constitution says and the Supreme Court interprets but only so much of each as 48 governors are willing to allow their sovereign domains. He has asserted a principle of anarchy incompatible with the idea of the United States.

IV

On Monday, September 9, six Negro students, accompanied by four Negro ministers, attempted to enroll in North Little Rock High School. A score of white youths, none of whom the school principal recognized as students, pushed the Negroes back from the entrance. Police and a few state troopers took up positions at the school and the Negroes abandoned their efforts to enroll.

About the same time, the crowd of around 150 persons that continued to collect daily outside Central High School threatened a Negro reporter for a New York newspaper. Guardsmen protected the reporter and an officer later took him away in an automobile while the demonstrators shouted:

"Let us at him! We'll take care of him!"

The crowd also heckled or threatened white reporters from various newspapers in northern states, including Benjamin Fine of the *New York Times,* who had been reprimanded by Colonel Marion E. Johnson for "inciting to riot" because a crowd collected when he went about his job of interviewing various anti-integration demonstrators. Members of the mob threatened news photographers on occasion and shouted at the reporters to "go back where you belong."

Later on Monday—the ninety-fourth anniversary, incidentally, of the invasion of Little Rock by federal troops during the Civil War—word came from President Eisenhower's vacation headquarters at Newport, Rhode Island, that legal proceedings would be initiated to force Faubus to cease interference with the integration of Central High School. At the same time, the FBI's four-hundred-page formal report on its investigations into responsibility for the developments at the school was delivered by U.S. District Attorney Orso Cobb to Judge Davies.

The Judge promptly ordered Cobb and Attorney General Herbert Brownell, Jr., to file a petition for an injunction against the Governor, Major General Sherman T. Clinger, the state adjutant general, and Lieutenant Colonel Marion E. Johnson, commander at Central High School. Faubus and the two National Guard officers were ordered to appear in federal court on September 20 for a hearing. In Washington, Deputy Attorney General William P. Rogers made it clear to newspapermen that the federal government's participation was strictly at the behest of the Judge.

For the next ten days, classes continued in nightmarish fashion at Central High School while the politicians and the propagandists and the newspapers had a field day. Everybody wanted to get into the act. A Congressman quoted President Eisenhower as saying that "patience is the important thing." Secretary of State John Foster Dulles warned that Communists abroad were using the Little Rock crisis as propaganda to make the United States look bad. Governor Faubus declared the federal government was alarming many Americans by usurping rights reserved to the states. Governor Marvin Griffin of Georgia declared that segregation and nothing else was the issue and that Faubus was on sound ground. Senator Hubert Humphrey of Minnesota called on Mr. Eisenhower to go to Little Rock and "personally take those colored children by the hand and lead them into school where they belong." A beer parlor waitress named Louise led a crowd of several hundred persons outside Central High School in jeering at a Jewish reporter and shouting that he was a "nigger-lover writing for those nigger papers up north." A previously dignified theater audience at Westbury, N.Y., disrupted a performance of the musical *South Pacific* by booing vigorously when the heroine—Nellie Forbush, played by Fran Warren—reached a line in the script that required her to say she came from Little Rock, Arkansas.

On Wednesday, September 11, after consultations with Congressman Brooks Hays of Little Rock, Governor Faubus sent a telegram to the President saying that "all good citizens must, of course, obey all proper orders of our courts" and suggesting that they "counsel together" in determining his course of action as chief executive of Arkansas. Mr. Eisenhower invited Faubus and Hays to confer at Newport that weekend.

I had no personal knowledge of the conference between the President and Governor Faubus other than what I read in the newspapers. On Saturday, after what was called a "constructive" meeting, the Governor issued a statement saying, with certain reservations, he had assured Mr. Eisenhower of his desire to be co-operative and that he regarded the Supreme Court decisions on integration of schools as "the law of the land" and the law "must be obeyed." "The people of Little Rock," he added, "are law abiding and I know that they expect to obey valid court orders. In this they shall have my support." The President announced that Faubus had stated his intention "to respect the decisions . . . and to give his full co-operation in carrying out his responsibilities in respect to these decisions."

These statements at first glance seemed encouraging, but in fact they solved nothing. One veteran White House reporter, Merriman Smith of the United Press, wrote that Faubus had asked the President for a one-year "cooling-off" period after which he would co-operate in preparing the people to accept integration. Faubus, according to remarks later attributed to him by the New York *Herald Tribune*, felt that the President was impressed by this proposal because he called in Attorney General Brownell and asked what could be done to give Little Rock authorities more time. Brownell was quoted as saying that nothing could be done.

While the Governor was still at Newport he said the National Guard would remain on duty around Central High School. A reporter then asked him if his meeting with the President had changed the Little Rock situation. Faubus replied: "I wouldn't know."

V

Faubus didn't know. The President apparently didn't know. Congressman Hays didn't know. Nobody knew. Hays spent the next few days, after their return to Little Rock, in prolonged conference with the Governor, trying to reach some compromise before the injunction hearing scheduled by Judge Davies for the following Friday, September 20. The effort failed.

On Friday, a tense crowd packed Judge Davies' courtroom. A small, vigorous man with a square face and smooth hair parted in the middle, Davies conducted the hearing briskly and with a kind of peppery humor. He began by hearing a series of motions by attorneys for Faubus, who was not present, designed to delay the proceedings or to persuade the Judge to disqualify himself. The maneuvers dragged on for more than an hour, with the Judge overruling all of the motions.

Finally, one Faubus lawyer, Tom Harper, asked whether all preliminary matters had been disposed of prior to calling witnesses, Davies snapped: "I think so."

"The position of the respondent, Governor Faubus . . . must be firm, unequivocal, unalterable," Harper then said, bringing up the legal grounds on which Faubus based his actions. The Governor of the state of Arkansas cannot and will not concede that the United States in this court or anywhere else can question his discretion and judgment as chief executive of a sovereign state when he acts in the performance of his constitutional duties."

This did not mean, he added, that Faubus would not comply —at least pending appeal—with any orders the court might give. Then he shocked the federal lawyers by saying the Governor's attorneys could proceed no further and asking the Judge to excuse them. This unusual request was granted and they walked out. Thus they avoided having to try to answer witnesses who later testified that there had been no need for calling out the National Guard to maintain order.

The Department of Justice lawyers had more than one hundred witnesses available and also had the bulky report by the FBI on responsibility for interference with integration at Central High School. The report was not made public and only eight witnesses were called to testify. They included school officials, two Negro students, General Clinger, Police Chief Potts and Mayor Mann.

My testimony concerned the plan for integration. I said the plan was "very well accepted" by the students. The majority of the people of Little Rock did not want integration, I added, but "they favor this plan as the best answer to a difficult problem."

When General Clinger testified, U.S. Attorney Cobb asked him if the National Guard was stationed at Central High School to "keep Negroes out of the school."

"Now, don't get me in bad with my commander-in-chief," the General said, objecting to the form of the question.

Cobb then asked if the Guard had been used to carry out the Governor's order to put white schools off limits to Negroes and Negro schools off limits to whites.

"Yes," Clinger replied.

Incidentally, the text of Faubus' orders to General Clinger, as revealed later, said: "You are directed to place off limits to white students these schools for colored students and to place off limits to colored students these schools heretofore operated and recently set up for white students. This order will remain in effect until the demobilization of the guard or until further orders."

Another witness at the hearing, Mayor Mann, testified that "we didn't believe" the situation at the school would get out of hand and that he knew of no incidents of racial violence in Little Rock in the past twenty-five years. Police Chief Potts gave about the same testimony. Dr. Cooper, president of the School Board, was asked if the community had accepted the integration plan.

"The great majority of the people approved the plan," he replied. "Some thought it too slow and some thought we should have no plan at all."

Clark Eardley, a Justice Department lawyer, said in summing up that "no reasonable person" could believe that the plan would cause racial violence. Governor Faubus, he concluded, had acted arbitrarily and summarily to keep the Negro children from "exercising their constitutional rights."

The decision of Judge Davies asserted that "it is . . . demonstrable from the testimony here today that there would have been no violence in carrying out the plan of integration, and there has been no violence." He declared that the court-approved plan for gradual integration had been "thwarted" by the Governor's use of the National Guard. The Judge then granted the government's request for an injunction and ordered Faubus to cease interfering with integration at Central High School.

Late that same afternoon, the National Guard moved out of the school grounds on orders from Governor Faubus, who promptly left town to attend the Southern Governors Conference at Sea Island, Georgia.

We had until Monday—less than three days—to prepare for nine Negro students to enter Central High School.

Chapter Eight

BLACK MONDAY

OVER THE WEEKEND of September 21, students at Central High had a chance to read the first issue of the term of *The Tiger*, a student publication. And they had a chance to read an editorial that had been written by Jane Emery, a co-editor. It said:

You are being watched! Today the world is watching you, the students of Central High. They want to know what your reactions, behavior and impulses will be concerning a matter now before us. After all, as we see it, it settles now to a matter of interpretation of law and order.

Will you be stubborn, obstinate, or refuse to listen to both sides of the question? Will your knowledge of science help you determine your action or will you let customs, superstition or tradition determine the decision for you?

This is the chance that the youth of America has been waiting for. Through an open mind, broad outlook, wise thinking and a careful choice you can prove that America's youth has not "gone to the dogs," that their moral, spiritual and educational standards are not being lowered. This is the opportunity for you as citizens of Arkansas and students of Little Rock Central High to show the world that Arkansas is a progressive, thriving state of wide-awake alert people. It is a state

99

which is rapidly growing and improving its social, health and educational facilities. That it is a state with friendly, happy and conscientious citizens who love and cherish their freedom.

It has been said that life is just a chain of problems. If this is true, then this experience in making up your own mind and determining right from wrong will be of great value to you in life.

The challenge is yours, as future adults of America, to prove your maturity, intelligence and ability to make decisions by how you react, behave and conduct yourself in this controversial question. What is your answer to this challenge?

Students also had an opportunity that weekend to read an advertisement paid for by the Capital Citizens' Council urging "all . . . who are against race-mixing in our schools" to attend a public meeting on Tuesday night. Amis Guthridge, attorney for the Council, said that he had heard the police planned to escort Negro students to school on Monday and that anybody getting in the way "will get their heads beaten."

"It seems that the stage is set for the Communist Party's finest hour in trying to incite trouble," he added, according to newspaper accounts. "If violence comes, the blame will be on a small clique of white revolutionaries who, while supported with money from tax-exempt rich foundations, have engineered the whole thing. If the communists and the NAACP are to be our overlords and masters under a police state, we might as well find out now as a little later."

There was other reading matter that weekend. Little Rock was flooded by a mass of segregationist and anti-Semitic literature.

II

My administrative staff worked closely with the police throughout the weekend to complete preparations for entry of the Negro students into the school, and with approval of the School Board I issued a statement asking all adults not employed there to remain away from the school on Monday. "We do not know when the Negro students will come to classes," I added. "The school will be open to all on Monday."

Mayor Mann, taking up the role of "preservator" of the peace, urged all citizens to accept integration and warned that city law-enforcement officers would be ready to deal firmly with those "who might try to create trouble." About one hundred city police and fifty-four state police were detailed to the school area, which meant some city patrolmen would be virtually on day and night duty.

The School Board instructed me also to seek the assistance of United States marshals. I telephoned Judge Davies and he told me such a request should be made through U.S. Marshal-in-charge Beall Kidd. I then advised Kidd that the Board requested the presence of enough marshals to assure that the children could safely enter the school. He said he would take up the request formally with Judge Davies. About an hour later, Kidd telephoned to tell me that it would not be possible to provide any marshals for duty at the school. In other words, the federal government was still handing out court decrees but doing nothing to assist local efforts to enforce the court's orders.

This unhappy attitude was further emphasized by two statements from President Eisenhower at his vacation headquarters at Newport, R.I. He said he was confident that the people of Little Rock would "vigorously oppose any violence by extremists" and that the withdrawal of National Guard troops by Faubus was "a necessary step in the right direction." He made it clear that the problem was "now in the hands of local enforcement authorities."

The President praised the attitude of the Negro students who had been barred from the school, and said they and their parents acted with "dignity and restraint. All parents must have a sympathetic understanding of the ordeal to which the nine Negro children . . . have been subjected."

At Sea Island Governor Faubus was quoted by reporters as saying that he hoped all would be well but that he thought there would be violence if Negroes entered Central High School. In that event, he added, it would be up to Lieutenant Governor Nathan Gordon to "use his own judgment" as to whether the National Guard should be called out again. The next day, Sunday, he charged that the city officials of Little Rock and the *Arkansas Gazette* were conspiring to "crucify" him. He referred to a report that city officials had asked the Lieutenant Governor to put the National Guard on a stand-by basis and then withdrawn the request. "That indicates the kind of game they're playing—these men who testified in court that there would be no violence," he added. He said he was greatly pleased by the public support he had received and, according to one reporter, implied that he might run for a third term.

Mayor Mann, in a statement, said that "a strong police detail will be on hand at Central High School to deal with any efforts by mob leaders to breach the peace of this community. Arrangements have been made for additional assistance if that becomes necessary. Violations of city ordinances and state laws will be dealt with firmly. . . . It is my sincere hope that our citizens will co-operate with the city police as they fulfill the responsibilities imposed on them by law."

The Little Rock newspapers carried editorial appeals to citizens to remember that the world would be watching their conduct. "Our one wise course for the present," said the *Arkansas Democrat*, "is to maintain a calm atmosphere, going quietly about our affairs, holding back hot, angry words and giving no support to disorder, however we may sympathize with its motive."

Ministers throughout the city offered prayers for peace. Mrs. Margaret Jackson, a vice-president of the Mothers League, was quoted in the newspapers as saying "we hope to have a big demonstration on Monday to show that the people of Little Rock are still against integration and I hope they [the Negro students] won't get in." But leaders of the Capital Citizens' Council said they were opposed to violence. In fact, it was a quiet, if nervous, weekend except for an anonymous note received by the Mayor: SEE YOU LATER, INTEGRATOR!

III

Early Monday morning I drove past Central High School en route to my midtown office. The police were on duty under direction of Assistant Chief Gene Smith and a crowd was beginning to form outside the barricades erected at strategic points. I had arranged to keep closely in touch by telephone with Smith and with Principal Jess Matthews, as well as with the Mayor and Chief Potts, who were at City Hall, and I received a running account of developments during the day.

As reported later by police and newspaper reporters, the crowd had grown to more than a thousand by 8 A.M. and Smith noted that many of them arrived in automobiles bearing license plates that showed they came from counties elsewhere in the state. I was pleased to have Gene Smith in charge of the police at the school. A big, active man standing around six feet, two inches, he was a graduate of Central High School, where he had been a star athlete. He was friendly but forceful and respected by his men. He had a well-earned reputation as a fearless police officer, and not long before, when a man had gone berserk and holed up in a house with a gun, it was Smith who went into the house and brought him out. I thought that with Smith in charge the police would do a good job that day even though I knew they were overwhelmingly opposed to integration. I was not disappointed.

The atmosphere was ominous as the first white students passed through the police barricades and entered the school building, which is set well back from the street on grounds that run two city blocks along Park Avenue. At a quarter of nine, just as classes were starting, a local news photographer saw a Negro boy and a Negro man walking along an adjacent street toward the school, some distance from the police lines.

"Here they come!" a white man near the corner yelled. He and several companions ran toward the Negroes. The boy ran away but the Negro man did not run. He was knocked to the street and a white man kicked him in the face as the photographer watched. The group forced the Negro back down the street and a white man carrying a heavy rock said: "I'm going to give you three minutes." The Negro never said a word.

At the same time, several Negro newspapermen appeared near the school and the mob surged around them. There were no police near.

"Go home you —— nigger!" somebody shouted. The reporters turned to leave but as they did so a white man shoved one of them and a moment later the Negroes were being pummeled and kicked. Two men dragged one of them into some high grass, kicked him and slugged him and smashed the camera he was carrying.

"Anybody got a rope?" a man in the crowd roared. "Let's hang 'em!"

"I can get one in a hurry," another replied.

The punching and kicking continued—one Negro was knocked down several times—as the victims retreated a block or more. Then the mob's attention was attracted away from them as a yell went up from in front of the school building: "Everybody here! The niggers are already inside. . . . Let's go get 'em!"

The eight Negro students—one who was eligible stayed away— had arrived quietly in automobiles at the south entrance of the building, accompanied by their parents. The adults drove away after the children had gone inside without being seen by the crowd.

Angrily shouting, "Let's go in!" the mob ran around the building and surged against the police lines. A woman screamed: "I want my child out of there!" There was confusion at several points as the most vociferous agitators—some of whom Smith definitely identified as being from other towns—encouraged the demonstrators to break through the police barricades. Slowly the police fell back to the sidewalk in front of the school, but there they began using their clubs when necessary. One man grabbed Smith by the collar. "What about it, Gene?" he yelled. "Did you let the niggers in when you were in school here?"

"Let's go home and get our shotguns," another man suggested.

"I hope," a woman shouted, "they drag out eight dead niggers!" Smith and his men stood firm. "I don't want to hurt anybody," the Assistant Chief said, but when one of the out-of-town demonstrators—a big, roaring man—charged the police so hard it took four men to stop him, Smith grabbed a club and knocked him down. The felled man and another agitator were loaded into a police van and driven away. The firmness of the police quickly cooled off demonstrators who wanted to get into the school, but the shouts and jeers continued as the crowd was forced back and one man was arrested.

"You Communists!" some bystanders yelled at police. Two officers asked a middle-aged woman to move back and, when she twice refused, they bundled her into a police car. Whenever the demonstrators saw white students at the windows, they shouted for them to walk out of school. One city patrolman, presumably unhappy with his assignment, turned his badge over to his lieutenant and walked off the job.

"You all ought to do the same," spectators shouted to the police and took up a collection of about $140 for the man who quit his job. About twenty-five persons were arrested during the day, and others were taken into custody that night and the next day.

Several young people, including one girl student, were among those arrested by police, and some of their friends went to City Hall to demand their release. Eight boys drove up to one side of the building yelling "Nigger lovers!" and shouting to their companions inside. "Let's go and get them out," they yelled, but as soon as a policeman walked to the window and looked out at them they got back into their car and drove away.

Later, during a court action, Smith gave his own impressions of the disturbance in answers to questions by lawyers:

Q. Would you please explain the attitude of the mob.

A. Well, there was a lot of profanity used toward the police department. People were saying that Negroes had better schools, why should they be there. There was talk of going inside and getting them out, talk and shouts, "Let's go in and get the Negroes out of the school."

Q. Were the members of your force abused by this mob in the language they used?

A. Yes, sir.

Q. How did the mob act?

A. Well, they tried to break through our barricades several times, and one or two of them broke through, or three or four at a time, and would be pushed back.

Q. Did you recognize any of the people who were forming into the mob.

A. Yes, sir. . . . We noticed cars from out of town coming in. I recall the numerals. They were from Pine Bluff and Benton. I noticed cars around the school. They were not Pulaski County cars.

(The witness was shown a photograph of several rioters)

A. I can't recall their names. The picture there—the man with the big hat—is from Benton. He was one of the trouble-makers, agitators, wanted to go into the school and trying to get the mob to follow them. This is the officer that pushed them back. And this picture is an individual having words, and shortly before that I had been grabbed by the tie, and I pushed a man back and he was threatening. I said let go or I will hit you, and this fellow came up and we had a few words back and forth.

Five newspapermen, including two photographers, all of them from out of town, were attacked by angry demonstrators during the rioting and chased behind the police lines. One was slugged in the mouth, another had a cut on his neck and a third was kicked and had his shirt torn off. Police took them to the station in automobiles that were showered with rocks.

The crowds frequently cheered when they saw a white student come out of the building and walk away. The school telephone switchboard was swamped by calls from parents demanding that their children be sent home. Most of them were afraid of violence, but some said they wanted their children to leave as a protest against admission of Negroes.

At one point, two white girls walked out of the building with tears streaming down their faces, saying: "They're in. They're in!"

Two Negroes driving a truck on a nearby street were surrounded by the mob. Demonstrators reached through the windows to strike at the occupants and tried to overturn the truck. Its windows were smashed with rocks before the Negroes could drive away. A Negro who drove into a nearby service station was rushed by several men but he jumped back in his car and left hurriedly as police intervened.

"Wails of hysterical women and fearful threats of men charged the tense air," wrote Phyllis Dillaha in the *Arkansas Democrat*. "The Central High School scene was marked by chaos and frustrated anger."

IV

Despite the uproar on the outside, there was no serious trouble when the Negro students attended classes inside the building. As school officials reported to me later, a small percentage of children—it was not possible to know just how many—walked out of various classes. In one class, two or three white students walked out when a Negro student was seated. In another class, almost half the white students walked out. There was a good deal of noise in the halls.

Terrance Roberts, one of the Negro students, said later that "there was not a whole lot of trouble. I was pushed but I don't know that anybody got hit. It was quiet after we got into classes. Some of the white students walked out. Just a few."

Slurring remarks were occasionally made to the Negro students and sometimes several boys would block the passage of a Negro boy or girl through a doorway. One white girl slapped a Negro girl, who turned and said, "Thank you," and then walked on down the hall. A dozen white girls walked out when a Negro girl signed up for their gym class. On the other hand, many students spoke words of welcome and encouragement to the Negro children and urged them to "stay and fight it out." One white girl later told reporters there was "very little trouble at all" and that most of her classmates were "disgusted" with students who walked out. Other students said that they left because their parents had told them to leave if most of their classmates walked out.

About an hour after classes started I received a telephone call from Mayor Mann expressing alarm and suggesting the Negro students be removed.

"Why?" I asked.

"There'll be a riot," he said.

"Let's get Gene Smith's opinion," I said. "If he says the Negroes should be removed for the safety of all, I'll agree."

An hour later, the Mayor called again, and renewed his suggestion. I telephoned the Assistant Chief of Police at the school about eleven-thirty.

"We've got things under control," Smith told me, "but if the crowd keeps on growing it could be difficult."

"What about the lunch hour when classes are out—or after school?"

"That's what is worrying me," Smith replied. "Some of these people might try to follow the Negro students home. It might be wise to take them out now."

"All right," I said. "Go ahead and do it."

Just before noon, school officials told the Negro students it had been decided to take them home for safety's sake. None objected. They left by a back door and were driven away before the crowd knew what was happening. In fact, the demonstrators refused to believe the police announcement that they had been taken home. They demanded that they be permitted to go inside the building to see for themselves. Finally, the police selected a woman from the crowd and took her inside. She returned and reported there was no trace of the Negro students.

Still the crowd was not satisfied. Some drifted away during the early afternoon when the school registrar came out and announced over the loudspeaker that the Negroes had been "sent home and have been withdrawn." But there were still quite a few in the street when school was dismissed and the students—about 450 were absent or had walked out—came out of the building.

Most of them went directly home, but there were a few groups who yelled at the spectators and danced around in the street, singing:

> Two!—four!—six!—EIGHT!
> We ain't gonna inteGRATE!

Chapter Nine

THE PRESIDENT'S HOUR OF DECISION

WE WERE A DIVIDED city on Monday evening, September 23—and, for the moment at least, I was losing hope for a calm and intelligent solution of the problem of school integration. There were, of course, men and women—then and later—who sought a sane method of procedure. Yet the efforts of the moderates always seemed to backfire and make our situation worse instead of better, while Governor Faubus appeared to be able to capitalize on every development to strengthen his position with the people of Arkansas.

In other words, sentiment in favor of the School Board's plan of integration lost ground steadily, as was later pointed out in court testimony by Wayne Upton, a prominent lawyer, who was then secretary of the Board and later became president:

Q. Mr. Upton, before September of 1957, did you have any occasion to discuss the integration problem with people in Little Rock?
A. I discussed the problem generally with a great number of people. . . . The people that I came in contact with generally, after the School Board's plan had been announced, seemed to think that, while maybe that particular person was not in favor of integration, the

School Board's plan was sound and was workable and it afforded us a means of meeting the requirements of the law with a limited amount of integration. . . .

Q. Since September, 1957, have people discussed this problem with you generally at length?

A. At greater length than I would like on many, many occasions, considering that I have other things to do, and a very great number of them expressed a great deal of displeasure at what the School Board had done and what they had gotten us into, and expressed the feeling and hoped that after all there was a way out of this. . . . [Their feelings were that] if the people of the state didn't want integration they ought not to have to submit to it, and the general feeling was that an order of the United States Supreme Court is not the law—can't be the law. . . . There was quite a marked change . . . on the part of the people who had previously apparently felt the other way, [but now] thought the School Board had not done all it could to prevent integration, and that we didn't have to have integration.

Q. Generally, were those fairly intelligent people . . . ?

A. Yes.

II

While the mob was still outside Central High School on Monday afternoon, Governor Faubus told the *Arkansas Democrat* by telephone from Sea Island that city and school officials and Negro leaders "should have the good sense to do what I urged them to do—allow for a cooling off period. I think this could have been worse the first day [of school] and because I didn't want this to happen I acted the way I did in calling out the National Guard. I wanted to avoid this sort of thing—this violence. It is repulsive to me to have it happen in my state."

The disorders also brought action from President Eisenhower at Newport, where he issued a warning statement:

I want to make several things very clear in connection with the disgraceful occurrences today at Central High School in the City of Little Rock.

1—The federal law and orders of the United States district court implementing that law cannot be flouted with impunity by any individual or any mob extremists.

2—I will use the full power of the United States—including whatever force may be necessary—to prevent any obstruction of the law and to carry out the orders of the federal court.

3—Of course every right thinking citizen will hope that the American sense of justice and fair play will prevail in this case. It will be a sad day for this country—both at home and abroad—if school children can safely attend their classes only under the protection of armed guards.

4—I repeat my expressed confidence that the citizens of Little Rock and or Arkansas will respect the law and will not countenance violations of law and order by extremists.

The President then signed a proclamation stating that

"certain persons in the State of Arkansas, individually and in unlawful assemblages, combinations and conspiracies, have willfully obstructed the enforcement of orders of the United States District Court . . . with respect to enrollment and attendance at public schools." Such obstruction, the proclamation continued, impeded the course of justice and "therefore, I, Dwight D. Eisenhower, President of the United States, under and by virtue of the authority vested in me . . . do command all persons engaged in such obstruction of justice to cease and desist therefrom and to disperse forthwith."

Anticipating drastic federal action, Governor Faubus and Arkansas's Senator John L. McClellan challenged the authority of the President to use federal troops to enforce integration. Dispatches quoted the Governor as saying federal troops could not be used unless he asked for them and "I don't plan to make any such request. It is clearly defined under the constitution and the law that the forces of the federal government cannot be employed except on request of the governor of a sovereign state. I agree that it is a sad day when you can attend school only under armed guard. But if the President will leave it to Lieutenant Governor Gordon or myself the responsibility for the maintenance of peace and good order it will be preserved."

Governor Theodore McKeldin of Maryland, a Republican, also at Sea Island, commented that Faubus "wrote the book, set the stage and directed the plan for today's unhappy occurrences. Even across the miles from Sea Island he gave the cues to his players in screaming headlines predicting violence." Mayor Mann charged that the mob was "agitated, aroused and assembled by a concerted plan. It bore all the marks of the professional agitator."

On Tuesday morning, about two hundred persons again gathered outside Central High School, but the Negro students did not appear and Mrs. Daisy Bates said they would not return until assured of adequate protection. About seven hundred white students also were absent. Police arrested nine persons—two carrying weapons—at the school, and seized forty-five others around the city in isolated cases of vandalism and racial violence.

There was some unusual activity at City Hall Tuesday morning, too, but I did not learn about it until later. Mayor Mann, according to his own account much later, put in a telephone call for the White House and, although he didn't get the President, talked to Maxwell Rabb, the presidential assistant on minority matters. He told Rabb that the situation in Little Rock was no better, that the mob was growing, singing and chanting obscenities, and that a slight incident might touch off bloodshed.

Rabb replied, according to the Mayor, that Brownell understood the seriousness of the situation, and suggested that Mann be ready to send a telegram to the President asking for federal troops. The two talked by telephone several times and the Mayor read a telegram he had prepared. Rabb suggested a few minor changes and Mann then dispatched the message to Mr. Eisenhower. It said that "the immediate need for federal troops is urgent. The mob is much larger. . . . People are converging on the scene from all directions. Mob is armed and engaged in fisticuffs and other acts of violence. Situation out of control and police cannot disperse the mob. I am pleading with you as President of the United States . . . to provide the necessary troops within several hours."

During the morning the President took a first ominous step by issuing an order federalizing the Arkansas National Guard—removing it from the control of Faubus and putting it under Army direction. Then, late in the afternoon, I received a call from the Arkansas Military Department of the U.S. Army asking me to come to the Military District offices at five-thirty. Just before dusk, I arrived at the offices in the center of town near the broad, concrete Broadway bridge over the Arkansas River. The place was buzzing with activity. A full staff was on duty, guards were on the doors and there was an air of tension. An unusual number of military vehicles were parked in the street and on an adjacent lot.

I identified myself and an aide escorted me to the office of Major General Edwin A. Walker, chief of the District. Walker, a tall, broad-shouldered Texan, had been stationed in Little Rock only a few months and I had met him only briefly, but I had been impressed by his erect, West Point bearing and his quiet but incisive manner of speech. He was always courteous and he evoked loyalty in those around him. Off duty, he was personable and pleasant but in uniform he was efficient and direct.

After greeting me, he motioned to a man in civilian clothes—a man as tall as Walker and as obviously a West Pointer.

"This is General Bus Wheeler," Walker said. I later learned that he was Major General Earle G. Wheeler, Assistant Deputy Chief of Staff for Military Operations at the Pentagon. Wheeler wasted no time in giving me the facts.

"A detachment of the 101st Airborne Infantry Division is moving in on orders directly from the President," he said. "They have already started landing at Little Rock Air Force Base and will soon be coming along there."

He pointed out the window to the Broadway bridge, a glimmering streak of lights in the growing darkness.

"Couldn't their entry be postponed at least until Thursday?" I asked. "The atmosphere here might be a bit calmer by then."

"No," Wheeler replied, "the orders from the President are to open the school for Negro students tomorrow and we will do it tomorrow. It is too late to try to get anything changed now.

"As we see it, this problem has two phases. One is psychological and one is real. There will be a certain number of what might be called sight-seers to handle. But there will be others ready to cause trouble. We have come with a lot more men than we will need and we will be able to exert absolute control of the situation. We don't want anybody hurt. We hope they will realize the extent of our strength and not try anything. But if some people have to be hurt I assure you it will be as few as possible."

There was a rumble of heavy wheels outside in the darkness and we turned to the window again. A city police car was leading a dozen jeeps and seven trucks carrying fully equipped white and Negro paratroopers—the men of the elite Screaming Eagle Division —across the Broadway bridge. Behind them came staff cars and other vehicles. The paratroopers brought everything with them from rifles and bayonets and billy clubs and gas masks to bedding and field kitchens. There was no doubt they meant business.

The grim procession could be seen in sharp outline as the vehicles lumbered past a huge and brightly lighted commercial billboard on which there was a map of our state and the words: "Who will build Arkansas if her own people do not?" I was thinking about those words when General Walker spoke again.

"How long," he asked, "do you think we will have to stay here?"

"Until such time," I replied, "as the persons who have made your presence necessary are indicted and brought to justice."

There was a brief silence in the room broken only by the distant noise of traffic across the bridge.

"Okay," General Wheeler said gravely. "We don't want to

hurt anybody, but those Negro students are going into that school. Where will we find them tomorrow morning?"

III

President Eisenhower told the nation by radio and television Tuesday evening his reasons for sending federal troops to Little Rock, saying in effect that mob action had endangered the safety of the United States and the free world.

". . . under the leadership of demagogic extremists," he said, "disorderly mobs have deliberately prevented the carrying out of proper orders from a federal court. . . . I yesterday issued a proclamation calling upon the mob to disperse. This morning the mob again gathered in front of the Central High School of Little Rock, obviously for the purpose of again preventing the carrying out of the Court's order in relation to the admission of Negro children to the school. . . .

"The interest of the nation in the proper fulfillment of the law's requirements cannot yield to opposition and demonstration by some few persons. Mob rule cannot be allowed to override the decisions of the courts. Let me make it very clear that federal troops are not being used to relieve local and state authorities of their primary duty to preserve the peace and order of the community. Nor are the troops there for the purpose of taking over responsibility of the School Board. . . . The troops are there pursuant to law solely for the purpose of preventing interference with the orders of the court. . . .

"At a time when we face a grave situation abroad because of the hatred that communism bears toward a system of government based on human rights, it would be difficult to exaggerate the harm that is being done to the prestige and influence, and indeed to the safety, of our nation and the world. . . .

"And so, with confidence, I call upon citizens of the State of Arkansas to assist in bringing to an immediate end all interference with the law and its processes . . . and Little Rock will return to its normal habits of peace and order and a blot upon the fair name and high honor of our nation in the world will be removed. Thus will be restored the image of America and of all its parts as one nation, indivisible, with liberty and justice for all."

Mr. Eisenhower's speech was backed up by news dispatches from Washington saying that the Department of Justice was sifting FBI reports for names of leaders of the mob and preparing to take action against them. The federal statutes, it was pointed out, provided a fine of $5,000 and five years in jail for convictions of conspiracy to injure, oppress or intimidate any citizen in the free exercise of any right or privilege secured to him by the Constitution or the laws of the United States. Congressman Kenneth B. Keating, a Republican from New York, called on the government to treat Faubus "just as it would any other lawbreaker." He said that Little Rock developments demonstrated the need for stronger legislation giving the Department of Justice power to instigate action against violators of civil rights. A Little Rock municipal judge warned that he would be so tough with persons arrested for creating racial trouble that "they may wish they were being tried by the Yankee judge in federal court." Police Chief Potts issued thirty shotguns to night patrolmen in the city and instructed them to put down all lawless acts.

Governor Faubus flew back to Little Rock during the afternoon, prior to the arrival of the paratroopers, and remarked to reporters that Mr. Eisenhower had used "bad judgment" in federalizing the Arkansas National Guard and taking them out of the Governor's hands. "I feel like General MacArthur," he added. "I have been relieved." Then he went to the executive mansion and remained silent as the 101st Division rolled into the city.

The troops had flown from Fort Campbell, Kentucky, in fifty-two C-123 and C-130 planes and landed at Little Rock Air Force Base. By nightfall they had surrounded Central High School. Their troop commander, Colonel Will A. Kuehn, consulted with

Assistant Police Chief Gene Smith as the soldiers piled out of jeeps and trucks. Negro soldiers in the detachment remained in their vehicles and continued to the Army Reserve Armory at Little Rock University. They were never used around the school. I was informed they would not be used anywhere unless it was necessary to protect Negro children at their homes.

Meantime, at General Walker's request I had arranged for the nine Negro students to gather at one home where they could be picked up by soldiers the next morning and escorted to the school. Mrs. Bates, as state president of the NAACP, had made arrangements with the children in the past and I telephoned her late in the evening, informing her that the nine were to be taken to school the next day.

"Oh, no," she replied. "I have told them they would not go until the following day. We had a meeting about it."

"Well, the orders come from the President and the Army says the children will be taken to school in the morning," I told her. "You must have them ready."

"I can't do it!"

"In the circumstances," I said, "you'll have to do it."

The line was silent for a few moments, and then she said she would advise the children to be ready.

While all this was going on, there was a meeting at a downtown hotel of about seven hundred members and supporters of the Capital Citizens' Council. The audience cheered a speaker who referred to Governor Faubus' action in using the National Guard to prevent integration. The Rev. Wesley Pruden was quoted by reporters as saying that Southerners may as well make up their minds that "the Communist Supreme Court will keep after us and the South will continue fighting." A petition was circulated for the recall of the Mayor and top police officials and a resolution was adopted asking Faubus to summon a special session of the Legislature to abolish the public school system.

But the echo of the 101st Division trucks rumbling through

the city streets may have affected the attitude of the extremists and the meeting, as one reporter put it, was "surprisingly moderate" in tone. One of the Army's crack outfits, including combat veterans who had fought at the Battle of the Bulge in World War II, was in town, and the segregation leaders were treading softly until they saw how the wind would blow.

Chapter Ten

INTEGRATION BY BAYONET

CENTRAL HIGH SCHOOL is a five-story building built on seven different levels and with six city blocks of lawn and athletic fields. Inside, many corridors are long and narrow and, in so large a building, difficult to supervise. I spent most of the night of Tuesday, September 24, talking with my administrative staff and Jess Matthews, the Central High principal, about the problem of protecting nine Negro students who would be widely scattered among some two thousand white pupils moving from class to class in all parts of the building. I ended up by writing a letter to General Walker suggesting various measures that should be taken for the protection of all students, including guards at the entrances and thirty guards in the various corridors. We also arranged to keep all unauthorized persons out by having teachers and students use their library cards as passes to the school.

On Wednesday morning sidewalk and street-corner barricades were erected and about 350 men of the 357th Airborne Battle Group took strategic positions around the school before the first "sight-seers" appeared in automobiles. As the soldiers kept traffic moving, one man stuck his head out of a car window and yelled: "Hi ya, Hitler!" It was significant that throughout the day most of the automobiles parked in the vicinity of the school were from outside Little Rock. A count showed twenty-five out-of-state cars and forty-two from other counties in Arkansas.

As the first spectators or demonstrators began to congregate they were photographed by military experts and watched by an Army helicopter that took off from the football field and hovered over the school all day, communicating by wireless with a command post Army truck in front of the building, and with jeeps that buzzed along the adjacent streets. Two soldiers with walkie-talkies were atop the school building. Newspaper reporters and photographers were permitted on the sidewalk across from the school, but all other civilians were told to move on. I was not at the school but later I received detailed reports on what happened from the school staff and the newspapers.

Shortly after eight o'clock a sergeant told a small group of teen-age boys to move away from one corner of the school area. They drifted a short distance and then stopped to talk to several young girls. One boy said, "If they don't have guards on them niggers in school, they'll get murdered." A lieutenant approached the group and said, "If you're students, go inside. If not, leave the area." The group, all of them students, shuffled their feet and did nothing.

The lieutenant motioned to a dozen soldiers on the corner, ordered them to point their bayonets straight ahead and walk. As they approached, the teen-agers turned and started moving away, but so slowly that the bayonets of the soldiers were only inches from the backs of two girls. The girls giggled and laughed and kept moving just fast enough, while alert news photographers snapped pictures of the scene. One of the photographs, taken at a slight angle, made it appear, incorrectly, that one of the girls was actually being prodded by a bayonet.

These photographs, incidentally, were later used with great effect in propaganda against the federal government. Congressmen and others said the South was outraged because the soldiers had bayonets on their guns. Segregationists circulated many thousands of small white cards with a crude drawing showing a small white child and a small Negro child being prodded together by the boots and bayonets of two big, fierce-looking soldiers. On the card were the words:

"Brotherhood by bayonet! Start loving each other—that's a court order."

So great was the furor aroused by this propaganda that a number of Southern members of Congress later telephoned me to ask whether the soldiers had tear gas equipment and whether "the Army brass is throwing its weight around down there." I replied that I didn't know whether they had tear gas but that their behavior was excellent.

But to get back to Tuesday's developments, it was just before nine-thirty that morning when an Army station wagon, followed by a jeep, screeched around the corner and stopped in front of the school. The helicopter circled overhead. The nine enrolled Negro students got out of the station wagon and, with twenty-two armed soldiers surrounding them, walked into the building. A few minutes later several white students walked out.

As the Negro students were arriving, a platoon of soldiers moving on the double—the paratroopers did everything on the double throughout the day—was summoned to a point a block away from the school to disperse a group of about one hundred persons. Most of them moved away, but a man from North Little Rock refused to leave the porch of a house. When a soldier approached, he was said to have grabbed the soldier's rifle. Two other soldiers quickly intervened and recovered the rifle, and one of them brought the butt of his own rifle up against the man's forehead, knocking him down. He got up with blood on his face, muttering: "I fought in the Marines. I never thought this would happen." The soldiers marched him away.

Another man—identified later as a native of another town—was jabbed in the arm with a bayonet when he refused to move promptly as ordered. A jeep with a loudspeaker rolled along the streets warning: "Return to your own homes immediately." Some men and women argued with the soldiers that they were on the private property of persons who had invited them to stand in the yard or on the porch, but they were forced to leave anyway. General Walker did not set any specific limits around the school building, but his soldiers generally kept crowds several blocks from the building. Twice the soldiers went to the rescue of Negro passersby who were threatened or chased by white youngsters.

Late in the morning, various knots of bystanders including some teen-age boys ignored several Army requests to move away. "We are now going to start making arrests," an officer announced over the loudspeaker. As soldiers advanced the boys ran, but the troops chased them and surrounded them with bayonets. A man and several boys were taken into custody. Another man who advanced on a sergeant ran into the flat side of a bayonet and was hit in the face with a rifle butt. He departed, bleeding. In all eight persons were held under arrest, the others being released by the soldiers. By noon the would-be demonstrators were fully convinced the troops meant business, and they melted away.

II

Inside the school there was comparative calm. Only 1,250 of the 2,000 students were present, but we knew that many had been kept at home because their parents feared there might be violence. The day began with General Walker addressing the student body. He said they had nothing to fear from the soldiers, but he warned that anyone who attempted to interfere with the proper administration of the school "will be removed by the soldiers." There would be no exceptions to enforcement of the law, he added, because "if it were otherwise we would not be a strong nation but a mere unruly mob."

There were some signs of hostility toward the Negroes in addition to a few walkouts. Several students whispered insults and otherwise made known their opposition to integration. But most of the students—I would say 95 percent—accepted the Negro pupils quietly and with dignity. I would like to emphasize that then and later during the year the student body displayed an attitude of good sense and good citizenship, with the exception of a small hard core of segregationist-minded boys and girls. These never numbered more than twenty-five or possibly fifty, and they were a small minority compared to the other students, many of whom went out of their way to make the Negroes welcome on the first full day of integration.

The only real incident occurred shortly before noon when an unidentified man or boy called the police and said a bomb had been planted in the building. This message was relayed to the school where a fire drill was ordered. All of the students marched outside and a number of white girls talked to one or two of the Negro girls while they waited on the lawn. One Negro girl told a reporter she was being "treated fine" and was making friends. Soldiers and school employees searched the building without finding a bomb and, after thirty-three minutes, the children returned to their classes. Later, the police received another bomb-scare telephone message, but this time the students were not removed. At the end of the school day, the Negro students were taken home in the Army station wagon with an escort of two jeeps loaded with soldiers.

In this way, Central High School was integrated—and our troubles began.

III

When I say our troubles began, I mean the troubles of the School Board and the school staff in trying to carry on a normal educational program while being harassed and obstructed by a small but growing minority that was aggressive and well organized. The segregationists were not long silent or inactive. And if the use of armed force in the controversy over integration of Central High School proved anything, it was that America's civil rights problem cannot be solved with bayonets.

Governor Faubus had been legally forced to abandon use of National Guard troops to thwart our plan for gradual integration. President Eisenhower had no choice but to send regular Army soldiers to protect Negro students from mob violence. But the fact that men of the elite 101st Airborne Infantry Division guarded the high school with bayonets fixed against civilian demonstrators was unfortunate, perhaps disastrous.

Since that time I have talked with many political leaders and government officials in all parts of the country and I believe the South's reaction to the use of federal troops at Little Rock was accurately summed up by a distinguished and moderate member of Congress who comes from a Southern state.

"When the President," he said, "sent the Army's toughest airborne troops with bayonets on their guns against unarmed white citizens he made a mistake for which he will never be forgiven. If the Army had used military police or even some ordinary outfit in the role of police they could have done the job—but you can't oppose even a minority of our citizens with bayonets as if you were fighting Nazi stormtroopers!"

I do not present this as an objective or unprejudiced reaction, but as a comment that reflected the attitude of many Southerners and accounted for increased opposition to desegregation in some states such as Arkansas. At the same time, I want to make clear that the 101st Airborne Division, while under orders to tolerate no monkey business, acted with circumspection and even tact in carrying out its unenviable assignment. As far as I was ever able to determine, the soldiers never trespassed on the stern orders laid down by General Walker, although there were occasions when they were taunted by students and there were several false charges made against them.

The charge that received the greatest publicity was made by Faubus, who asserted that he had information from parents that soldiers had followed girls into their dressing rooms at the school. He wrote a letter to General Walker, whom he addressed as the "Commander of the Occupation Forces." The General returned the letter unopened, but Faubus later released it to the newspapers:

> I have received a number of complaints from parents, mostly mothers, about your troops accompanying the girl students to their dressing rooms . . . this seems to me a wholly unwarranted and unnecessary action. . . . If the privacy of the girls' dressing rooms is to be invaded by federal troops, I am sure that it would appear more seemly to the people of this area if use were made of the Women's Army Corps, rather than male soldiers armed with rifles, bayonets and billy clubs. . . .
>
> If it appeared that the occupation of Central High School and Arkansas by federal troops were only temporary, then, perhaps, the citizens could endure the presence of your troops and the methods being used until the time of your departure. However, if federal troops are to remain as long as forcible integration of the school is necessary, then it is my opinion that you and your troops will be here for a long time.

The Governor's executive secretary, Arnold Sikes, told reporters that six girl students and two students' mothers had said it was true that the soldiers entered the girls' dressing rooms. In one instance, he said, he had been told that "the door was open and a soldier was standing at the door where they [the girls] were dressing. One of the girls was partially undressed."

These charges were thoroughly investigated by school authorities and by the Army. Assistant Superintendent Fred Graham said that the charge was "ridiculous." I issued a formal denial of the charge, and, after getting a report from General Walker, Army Secretary Wilbur M. Brucker said the charges were "an unworthy attempt to defame our American soldiers." The White House issued a statement saying that investigation showed the charges to be "vulgar and untrue." But, of course, the slander was widely circulated and helped to stir up resentment against the federal troops.

IV

Although the segregationists were momentarily thrown off balance by the vigorous efficiency of the paratroopers in demonstrating that violence would be a grave error, they quickly recovered and waited for their leaders to chart a new course of action.

On Thursday evening, September 26, Governor Faubus made his own views clear in a television broadcast to the nation in which he voiced bitter resentment of the "occupation" of Little Rock, although he also said the people should "go about our normal pursuits in a friendly, peaceful manner."

"We are now in occupied territory," the Governor said. "Evidence of the naked face of the federal government is here apparent in these unsheathed bayonets in the backs of school girls—in the backs of these students, in the bloody face of this railroad worker who was bayoneted and then felled by the butt of a rifle in the hands of a sergeant of the United States 101st Airborne Division."

Referring to his own wartime service in the 35th Division, which went to the relief of the 101st Division in the Battle of the Bulge, Faubus said that "today we find the members of the famed division, which I helped rescue, in Little Rock, Arkansas, bludgeoning innocent bystanders . . . and with the warm red blood of patriotic American citizens staining the cold, naked unsheathed knives. . . .

"Literally swarms of FBI agents have been operating throughout the city. Also, agents of the Counter Intelligence Corps and Criminal Investigative Division have been combing the area for days. Teen-age girls have been taken by the FBI and held incommunicado for hours of questioning while their frantic parents knew nothing of their whereabouts."

Faubus' reference to the FBI holding young girls incommunicado was promptly and vigorously denounced as a lie by J. Edgar Hoover, the FBI director.

The Governor also took a few cuts at Arkansans who had urged the people to maintain respect for the law, including Mayor Mann, former Governor McMath and Harry S. Ashmore, executive editor of the *Arkansas Gazette*. Ashmore, he said, had distorted the news; Mann had been repudiated by the people and the City Council; and McMath had been defeated disastrously at the polls. "These men and the few of their views," he continued, "are the ones who have sought to advise the President's 'palace guard' about the Little Rock situation. They bear a heavy responsibility for the unhappy events of the past few days. Would it not have been better for the President's advisors to listen to officials who have the people's confidence . . . ?

"While we are . . . an occupied area . . . we must endure as best we can. . . . I have been working and fighting for the right of my people to solve their problems peacefully. . . . I shall continue relentlessly on this course. . . .

"In the name of God, whom we all revere, in the name of liberty we hold so dear, in the name of decency, which we all cherish, what is happening in America? Is every right reserved to the states by the federal constitution now lost?

"Does the will of the people, that basic precept of democracy, no longer matter? Must the will of the majority now yield, under federal force, to the will of the minority regardless of consequences?

"If the answers to these questions are in the affirmative, then the basic principles of democracy are destroyed, and we no longer have a union of states under a republican form of government."

Faubus said that he had received "upwards of 100,000 letters and telegrams" from every state in the Union and that 95 to 98 per cent supported his efforts to "maintain the peace."

Segregationist leaders throughout Arkansas and the South were quick to follow up the theme that Faubus had expressed in his speech. Stickers appeared on automobiles on the theme: "I am a resident of occupied territory." According to news agency dispatches, Senator Herman Talmadge of Georgia described Mr. Eisenhower as "the conqueror of Little Rock" and said he wished he could cast a vote "for impeachment right now." He said the only answer for the South was to establish a private school system.

Senator Olin Johnston of South Carolina said that "if I were governor and [the President] came in, I'd give him a fight such as he has never been in. I'd proclaim a state of insurrection . . . and we'd find out who is going to run things." Senator Richard B. Russell of Georgia charged that totalitarian rule had been imposed on Arkansas and said, "It will have a calamitous effect on race relations and the cause of national unity." Russell sent a telegram to the President protesting "high handed and illegal methods being employed" by federal troops at Little Rock, and said that, if reports in the press were correct, these tactics "must have been copied from the manual issued the officers of Hitler's storm troopers."

There were, of course, many Congressmen and state officials in the North and in the border states who spoke up in support of Mr. Eisenhower, but the protest chorus was loudest and most acceptable to the ears of Southerners. Editorial comment in Arkansas newspapers generally deplored or strongly denounced the interference of the federal government and usually supported Faubus.

V

The Southern Governors Conference, which had been in session at Sea Island, initiated a move to heal the breach between Arkansas's capital and Washington. Governor LeRoy Collins, of Florida, newly elected chairman of the Conference, sent the

President a telegram saying that five of the governors had been named to a committee that sought a meeting with Mr. Eisenhower to discuss the earliest possible withdrawal of federal troops from Little Rock. The committee included Governor Luther H. Hodges of North Carolina, chairman; and Governors Frank Clement of Tennessee, Marvin Griffin of Georgia, Theodore R. McKeldin of Maryland and Collins.

Mr. Eisenhower replied that he would meet with the committee to discuss the subject of school integration generally. Four of the governors—Griffin did not go to Washington—met with the President on October 1, after having received from Faubus a statement that he would not obstruct orders of the federal courts, and that he would assume responsibility for maintaining law and order if federal troops were removed from Little Rock. This offered a basis for negotiation and the President agreed to go along.

"The President stated," according to a White House announcement, "that upon a declaration on the part of the governor of Arkansas that he will not obstruct the orders of the federal courts and . . . will maintain law and order, the President will direct the Secretary of Defense to return command of the Arkansas National Guard to the governor. Thereupon, as soon as practicable, all federal troops will be withdrawn."

This looked—for a few hours—like progress. Then Faubus issued the proposed declaration at Little Rock with a couple of words added. He said that "it has never been my intention to obstruct the orders of the federal courts, [and] the orders of the federal courts will not be obstructed by me. . . . This has been my stand and viewpoint throughout the controversy."

The words "by me" were not in the script that had been presented to the President, and the White House promptly said that the statement "does not constitute . . . the assurance that he intends to use his full powers as governor to prevent the obstruction of the orders of the United States District Court. . . . The President of the United States has no recourse at the present time except to maintain federal surveillance of the situation."

Governor McKeldin charged that Faubus had "double-crossed" the governors committee and "now stands as the only man of prominence in all America who wants the troops of the federal government kept in Little Rock. By his ignominious double-crossing of the sincere and serious governors . . . [he] has elected to pile infamy on the heap of disgrace which he has inflicted on the great state of Arkansas.

"Governor Faubus is no more opposed to interracial use of public school facilities than are the three governors who worked with me yesterday, and later with President Eisenhower and his aides. The difference is that Governors Collins, Hodges and Clement believe in constituted governments of law. Governor Faubus prefers the demagogue's dangerous and destructive appeal to the emotions of the mob."

VI

By this time, the segregationist leaders had revised their strategy and were busy with a new propaganda and pressure campaign. Basically, the new campaign was designed to create disorders and demonstrations by a minority of students inside Central High School, and thus make it difficult, if not impossible, to continue classes. They also set out, at the same time, to stir up public opinion in favor of closing down the school rather than permit it to continue on an integrated basis under guard of soldiers. The misleading argument was advanced that, if the school were closed, it could later be reopened as a private school on a segregated basis.

The campaign was begun with literature and newspaper advertisements such as this:

THIS IS AN APPEAL FOR HELP!
From the Vast Majority of the Citizens of Little Rock
to the Rest of the People of Arkansas

We ask you to contact your local state representatives and senators and tell them to urge Governor Faubus to call a special session of the

Legislature for the explicit purpose of withholding all state funds from Central High School. The school could later be opened as a private institution.

Please help us to end the federal conquest of our city and your state capital.

This Ad Paid for by 33 Law Abiding People in Little Rock.

The plea was taken up by speakers and some public officials, but at this time Faubus avoided calling a special session of the Legislature.

Chapter Eleven

THE HATE CAMPAIGN

THE FIRST SIGNS of organized resistance to federal troops began mildly enough near the end of the first week of what Governor Faubus had called the "occupation" of Little Rock. The Mothers League of Central High School appealed to the Governor to close the school, and the League's vice-president, Mrs. Margaret Jackson, said they had an "unquestionable right" to demand closure because the schools "are supported by our tax money."

"Federal dictatorship is not conducive to educational activities," she continued, "and we feel that the very lives of our children are in great danger in the school. They are attending classes under the watchful eyes of hardened soldiers, who are acting under stern orders."

Mrs. Jackson did not make clear just how this endangered the lives of students. As a matter of fact, the military had already begun to lessen the appearance of force by confining its activities to the immediate school grounds, by eliminating bayonets from rifles and by having guards inside the building leave their rifles elsewhere. Only a few paratroopers escorted the Negro students into the building after the first day and, within a short time, the escort to and from the school was abandoned.

133

I don't know whether these changes had a psychological effect on the segregationist-minded students, but on Friday a group of them greeted the arrival of the Negro students with shouts which the newspaper reporters variously described as "jeers" or "cheers." They were probably the former, because shortly thereafter some of the white students began a campaign of petty harassment of the Negroes inside the school. The trouble-makers, and again I want to emphasize that they were very few in number, began throwing pencils or pebbles at some of the Negroes as students thronged through the halls. There were also many opportunities for them to make remarks when the guards or teachers were out of earshot. For the most part the Negro students attempted to ignore such harassment, and the school staff repeatedly counseled them not to reply.

The following week a group of students formed a kind of blockade at the school entrance, apparently with the idea of obstructing the entry of the Negroes, but they were crossed up when the Negro students entered by a side door for the first time. A few yelling boys ran across the grounds to the side door, but there were no incidents.

At first these occurrences did not appear serious and we hoped they would cease as the students settled down to a more nearly normal routine. The school newspaper, *The Tiger*, carried editorials written by its student editors, urging the pupils to put aside their personal views on integration and try to make the most of their academic opportunities. *The Tiger* also pointed out, "just to keep the record straight," that less than one per cent of the population of Little Rock had been involved in the integration disturbances, and that many persons in the mob were not citizens of Little Rock. "Wouldn't it be better," the editorial asked, "for parents, townsmen and strangers to let the law take its course and seek a remedy for the situation in some other way?"

The attitude of most of the hard core of segregationist students did not improve, however, and as incidents increased the staff of

Central High School became more and more convinced that these troublemakers were being directly influenced by adults—not necessarily their parents—outside the school. In any event, the harassment of the Negro students was intensified, with several white boys and girls becoming identified as leaders in most of the incidents. These students took advantage of the fact that General Walker was attempting gradually to replace the Army paratroopers with soldiers of the federalized Arkansas Guard and, at first, the guardsmen were obviously less ready to act against demonstrators or trouble-makers. Later, their discipline was tightened.

On one occasion, a white boy blocked the sidewalk against Negro students entering the school, but they merely walked around him as Guardsmen hurried up to prevent trouble. Again, several boys walked past a Negro girl and a pile of books she carried flew up into the air. She picked them up and went on inside the school. A few minutes later, the arrival of General Walker was greeted with derisive rebel yells by students in front of the building. Inside the building, Negro students occasionally were pushed or kicked in the halls and two Negro boys were chased up a stairway before guardsmen intervened. Three white boys were suspended from school for such offenses.

Early in October, I was advised that members of the Mothers League had started an intensive telephone campaign to persuade parents to have their children join in a big "walkout" demonstration at the school. The rumor was circulated, according to some students, that Governor Faubus had said the school would have to close down if one-half or more of the students refused to attend classes. School attendance had been improving and more than 1,700 of the 2,000 students were in classes, and the Mothers League apparently felt some action was needed to prevent a return to normal.

On Thursday morning, 1,651 students reported for classes, but when the Negroes appeared about 85 boys and girls walked out despite warnings that they would be punished. Many of the students were placed in a difficult position by their parents, who had instructed them to walk out if a majority of their classmates left. The children were scattered in various rooms and naturally could not tell whether a "majority" walked out. Actually only a small percentage left most of the classes.

The students, except for a few leaders, showed no enthusiasm for the walkout and some of those who did leave treated it more or less as a joke. One boy who walked out paused at the door of his classroom and turned around to ask a friend why he wasn't leaving.

"Not me," the friend replied. "I'm chicken."

The other boy grinned and turned to a Negro boy seated nearby.

"Well, what about you?" he asked. "Are you walking out?"

"Not me," the Negro boy replied with a big grin. "I'm chicken, too."

A few of the walkout leaders wore Confederate caps or had Confederate flags pinned on their jackets. "Come on out, you chickens!" they cried as they went out the door. Outside about twenty-five adults were gathered on the sidewalk across the street. Some of the students ran behind a nearby house and came back with a straw-stuffed effigy of a Negro. One boy climbed a tree and hung the effigy from a limb with a rope and, as the crowd gathered around, it was set afire. Guardsmen pulled the figure down and slowly forced the crowd to disperse. One boy was arrested and, later, a girl student who taunted the soldiers was arrested.

Matthews, the school principal, advised me by telephone of the walkout. He said the leaders had been defiant and the students who walked out should be suspended. I agreed and all who walked out were suspended for three days. Some leaders were suspended for one or two weeks and a few were expelled for the rest of the year.

The evening of the unsuccessful walkout, I was interested in reading an article by Bobbie Forster, staff writer of the *Arkansas Democrat,* which indicated the strain—and sometimes the hysteria —in which parents and students were caught as a result of the conflict over integration. The article, in which I have eliminated the names, said:

A disturbed mother took her daughter home from Central High School today, with this statement:

"I'm all mixed up, and so is she."

The student, 15, a sophomore who joined the walkout from Central High today, was driving around one of the blocks near the school in a car with other teen-agers when her mother saw her, stopped the car and pulled her out.

The mother had been talking to newsmen about the walkout, and described her daughter as "a normal teen-ager, but she's all mixed up and I am, too. I will not let nine little colored students keep her from getting an education."

The daughter today was in a group of about 25 demonstrating students gathered in a soda fountain across the street from the school.

When the students left, the soldiers began moving them back toward the other protesting students. The daughter and another girl ran through a yard, the soldiers chasing after them.

"Leave me alone," the daughter screamed.

When she resisted, an officer ordered two soldiers to take her to the principal's office in the school.

"They're arresting me," the girl shrieked.

The officer insisted that she was not under arrest, but was removed "because she was agitating."

Four Guardsmen escorted the girl into the school. Later, she came out and told newsmen that the principal, J. W. Matthews, told her she would have to apply for readmission at the superintendent's office.

"I told him okay and walked out," the daughter said.

Asked if she would go back to school or stay at home, she answered: "I'll stay at home instead of going to school with Negroes."

The mother took her daughter's hand and said: "You will not stay at home. You're going to get an education."

II

Now, before I relate the more serious disturbances that developed inside Central High School during the late fall and early winter, I would like to explain how the community reacted to the presence of federal troops at Central High School and how that reaction affected integration.

There were many citizens of Little Rock who continued efforts to solve the integration problem peacefully. Congressman Hays was still seeking some formula for constructive action. About forty ministers of various churches met at the Trinity Episcopal Cathedral with the Right Reverend Robert R. Brown, Bishop of the Episcopal Diocese of Arkansas, to urge that special services be held to pray for "resistance" against unthinking agitators.

Bishop Paul Martin of the Methodist Church, Monsignor James E. O'Connell, representing Bishop Fletcher, Rabbi Ira Sanders, and Dr. Marion Boggs, pastor of the Second Presbyterian Church, spoke in favor of a city-wide Day of Prayer. The church leaders agreed that the prayers should be for support and preservation of law and order, for the leaders of the community, the state and the nation, for the youths in the schools of the community, for the casting out of rancor and prejudice in favor of understanding and compassion.

A group of twenty-four Baptist ministers of fundamentalist persuasion dissented from the plan and invited their congregations to pray for national leaders to be guided by constitutional law rather than by politics, for state leaders to be given wisdom and courage to fulfill their responsibilities to the citizens of Arkansas, and for all citizens to avoid overt acts "for which we would be sorry later." Since I have mentioned the Baptist Church earlier, I should add here that the Southern Baptist Convention was on record that "we recognize that this Supreme Court decision [on school integration] is in harmony with the constitutional guarantee of equal freedom to all citizens, and with Christian principles of equal justice and love for all men."

The Day of Prayer was approved in formal letters from President Eisenhower, Governor Faubus and the Little Rock School Board. It was observed in eighty-six churches on October 12. Churches were crowded, although no special campaign had been attempted to bring the people out. Later the church leaders attempted to arrange meetings for open-minded discussion of the integration problem. These were not particularly successful.

The church leaders and others continued to urge a reasonable and calm approach to a settlement of the school crisis that would permit withdrawal of the troops, but the people generally were not in a mood to listen to discussion of the issues if, indeed, they were willing to recognize the issues. The question of states' rights and respect for law and order had become so inextricably mixed and confused with the question of whether "niggers" could attend Central High School that calm discussion was almost impossible. Tempers flared. Old friends became embittered. Even members of families took different viewpoints. As a result, most citizens found it safer not to try to discuss the problem at all.

Meanwhile, the determined and well-organized segregationist minority was steaming up its new hate campaign against Army-enforced integration and, as the days rolled by, it seemed to attract more public attention and gain more support than did the peace-makers. Certainly, the methods used in the segregationist campaign were more likely to arouse emotions of anger and resentment than of calmness.

The literature that was circulated was designed to discredit federal officials and school officials as "race-mixers" and advocates of Communism. Some of it was crude—typewritten cards or cheap drawings on mimeographed sheets of paper—but much of it was handsomely printed and illustrated, and obviously a vast amount of money was being poured into the campaign.

One of the cards scattered throughout the city, for example, said:

PERMIT

Good Indefinitely

Bearer may freely and energetically kick the rumps of Virgil Blossom, Jess Matthews [C.H.S. principal], Harry Ashmore [of the *Arkansas Gazette*], Woodrow Mann . . . Daisy Bates and Archie House [School Board attorney], who conned me into goofing when I should have been golfing. Spiked shoes recommended.

(Signed) Dwight D. Eichenhauser

Goofus-in-chief.

Another card, printed in two colors, simply said: "Ike, go home! Liberation Day." Still another was inscribed: "Virgil Possum says: Call those chiggers—Che-grows." One card that was freely used listed my home telephone number, as well as the numbers of several other persons on the hate list, and encouraged people to call me as often as possible, especially in the middle of the night, and denounce integration or perhaps just curse.

Emblems inscribed "I like Faubus" and showing a picture of the Confederate flag were offered as badges or windshield stickers to persons who wanted to "let others know that you do not intend to dance to the tune of the NAACP. . . . Profit from the sale of these emblems will be used to help legally defend the constitutional rights of the states." Also on sale were rubber stamps with which envelopes could be decorated with a drawing of soldiers pushing two school girls with a bayonet, surrounded by the words: "Remember Little Rock!" Cards were freely handed around with such lines as: "If you believe in integration, take a nigger home to lunch—no, take two niggers home to lunch."

The segregationists frequently declared that they intended to make an "example" of me so that no other school superintendent would dare to favor any kind of integration plan. They tried about everything.

During this time, I became keenly aware that bigotry is a weapon that cuts in all directions. As the anti-integration propaganda increased, so did propaganda of an anti-Communist and anti-Semitic character until the result was an outpouring of hatred and venom, with all kinds of crackpots and hate peddlers trying to horn in. One product of the Association of Citizens' Councils of Arkansas included the following:

HAVE THE INTELLIGENTSIA OF AMERICA FALLEN VICTIM TO THE COMMUNISTIC PROGRAM FOR AMERICA?

To all appearances the Intelligentsia of our country, our smart people, the "eggheads," have been the most gullible in adopting the program laid out by the communists for the subjugation of America. It is they who have accepted the insidious plan of the United Educational and Scientific Organization (UNESCO), the educational branch of the United Nations, which is dominated by communistic influence. . . .

There is a well-designed and financed communistic plan now underway to destroy the South. The white people of the South will bear the brunt of this raid upon our rights and liberties. . . . This sinister plan is being aided by "fellow travelers" of our own race who are using the NAACP as a front to hide their nefarious activities. This is the first time in history that the people of any country have been forced, "at the point of the bayonet, the use of machineguns and tanks and the threat of the use of the atom bomb" to integrate with another race against their will. If this is to be, it might be that most of us would prefer the atom bomb. Be alert to the cunning methods now being used to brainwash you into accepting racial integration by theaters, radio, television, athletic events, newspapers and magazines.

The Association also put out a number of other tracts along similar lines under such headings as "The Fifth Column in America" and "Has Communism Engulfed Us Beyond the Point of Recall?" Pamphlets printed in other states, particularly Mississippi and Georgia, poured into Little Rock, quoting speeches and articles by segregationists such as Judge Tom P. Brady of Mississippi and the Rev. G. T. Gillespie, president emeritus of

Belhaven College at Jackson, Mississippi. Mr. Gillespie argued that "the rank and file of the Negro race are not particularly interested in intermarriage with the white race and if left to themselves would probably never seek it." Judge Brady quoted with enthusiasm a booklet published in Georgia that said: "Let it be known . . . that we in the South do not intend to obey men, however exalted their seats or black their robes or hearts. We intend to obey the laws of God. . . ."

III

The segregationists were prolific letter writers. My mail was full of denunciations day after day. The letters came from all over the country, although most of them were from Southern states. They rather monotonously repeated the segregationist propaganda with occasional variations. One extreme example was a letter from a woman, who obviously had money and social position, suggesting that the best solution to the school integration problem would be to have all Negroes "chained, piled in one huge pile and burned alive." While I am on the subject, I should mention that I also received many sympathetic and helpful letters from all over the country, including the South, plus a number of crackpot suggestions. A letter from a man in New York, for instance, said I could solve the entire problem by arranging for the teen-age daughters of a prominent white citizen of Little Rock to ride through the streets in a convertible with two Negro boys.

The parents of students at Central High School also were showered with propaganda and letters urging them to take their children out of school or to write to Faubus demanding a special session of the Legislature to close the school. The Women's Division of the White Citizens' Council circulated instructions on how to recruit new members, how to organize speeches at clubs and on the radio, how to get members to write letters to the newspapers, and how to weed out "undesirable" books in public and school libraries.

Meantime, there was a constant flow of letters to the newspapers along the lines of the following excerpts:

I, as a mother whose son gave his life in World War II for the freedom of the United States and the rights of its people, whose heart is so full of hurt and grief, feel that I must speak out against the use of America's own soldiers to force the will of a group of political figures upon the people of our land. Did my son die in vain, leaving his child and family stripped of all rights . . . to be dominated by a dictatorship of federal authorities . . . ?

I have been reading your column every day and some of the letters have made me furious. . . . In my opinion, Eisenhower hasn't the slightest notion of the situation in Arkansas. If he is such a great man, why does his granddaughter go to a private, all-white school . . . ? Why doesn't the great president come and live with Negroes in Arkansas for a while?

Many of the letters were more violent in language and, because the *Arkansas Gazette* had urged obedience to the law, the editors often were denounced. One woman wrote to the editor that she got madder and madder every time she picked up the paper and that she would have canceled her subscription long before except that in her continuing anger she had lost seven pounds. She ordered the newspaper continued until she had lost two more pounds.

Newspaper advertisements sponsored by segregationist organizations covered a wide field but, without much imagination, kept harping on such effective issues as "race-mixing" and the NAACP and action by the legislature to close Central High School. A few examples:

WHAT ARE THE "MODERATES" ADVOCATING—
RACE-MIXING?

The solution to the problem of States' Rights and Racial Integrity is to abide by the Constitution of the United States, not the Supreme

Court. The Supreme Court does not make the law!

The Citizens' Councils ask this question, "Where is the law regarding forced integration of the races? When was it passed and by whom?"

Now is the time to stand up and let your voice be heard. . . .

We urge the Governor to call a special session of the legislature immediately and to take the necessary action to retain the rights of this great state, and to keep for all peoples their God-given rights of freedom of choice, freedom of speech, and all liberties held dear by them and guaranteed to them under the Constitution of the United States.

The signature on the advertisement was the name of the Citizens' Council around a United States flag crossed with a Confederate banner. Another advertisement appealed for contributions to a "Freedom Fund" to provide legal defense for persons arrested during the disorders at the high school. One advertisement was published over the name of the Broadmoor Baptist Church, "paid for by Wesley Pruden," the pastor. It quoted "leading churchmen" who favored segregation and concluded with these words: "Our Lord was born into the most segregated race the world has ever known. Under this system He lived and died. Never did He lift His voice against segregation. Segregation has Christian sanction. Integration is Communistic."

In November of 1957, the Capital Citizens' Council branched out with some new scare ideas after Mrs. Edgar F. Dixon, a former member of the School Board, became a candidate for City Director under the new form of city manager government adopted in Little Rock. One of the Council's advertisements during the city election campaign said:

Do you want your police force further integrated?

Do you want Negro policemen arresting white people and hauling them into court?

Do you want your fire department integrated?

Do you want your swimming pools, parks and playgrounds integrated?

Do you want Negroes driving your city buses?

If not, defeat all candidates sponsored by the Good Government Committee.

Here are the facts:

Mrs. Edgar F. Dixon was a member of the Little Rock School Board when the Blossom plan was adopted . . . and is now running for City Director. Surely the people do not want that to happen in our city government that has happened at Central High School. . . .

In the election, incidentally, all but one of the Good Government Committee candidates were elected, but the races were so close that the result could not be regarded as indicating any decisive triumph for our school integration plan. In fact, the consensus was that the election showed much stronger anti-integration sentiment than existed before the school term opened.

Not a few of the advertisements during the last months of 1957 were personal attacks on me. One of them followed announcement that the School Board would not admit any additional Negro students to Central High School at the beginning of the next semester.

THANK YOU, MR. BLOSSOM

It was very kind of you to drop a crumb to the white people of Little Rock by assuring them that no Negroes would be admitted at midterm to Central High School. But, Mr. Blossom, if it is the 'law of the land' how can you refuse to admit them? We have heard so much of late about the much vaunted 'law of the land.' Last September you denied all responsibility in the matter of integration of Central High School, saying, "it is the law of the land, and we must be good citizens." Now you don't talk of the 'law of the land,' you tell us plainly that no more negroes are to be admitted this year. How can this be? Did the Supreme Court rule that only nine negroes were to have their so-called constitutional rights? Is it not true, Mr. Blossom, that you have stated that integration is regulated by the 'law of the land'?

Mr. Blossom, if you can manipulate this mythical 'law of the land' so as not to admit additional negro children at mid-term, why did you admit them last September 3? How about going one step further and assuring the people of Little Rock that no negroes will be in September of 1958, or at any time in the future. One other question—will any additional white children be admitted to Central High at mid-term? If so, is not this discrimination on the basis of color? And isn't this against the 'law of the land'?

Another similar personal attack was addressed to Matthews:

GOODBYE "WHITE CHRISTMAS"
AT CENTRAL HIGH SCHOOL

Mr. Jess Matthews, Principal,
Central High School
Dear sir,

The white parents of Little Rock stand amazed at the continuing outrages they and their children are being forced to submit to at the hands of our administration of Central High School. In particular, and with all the emphasis at our command, we resent and protest your action . . . in ordering the students not to sing the beautiful and time honored Christmas song, "White Christmas."

From numerous students we have learned that one of the negro girls complained to you that the singing of "White Christmas" by the students offended her tender sensibilities. On the basis of this complaint you were reported by the students to have banned the song. . . .

Mr. Matthews, we think you owe the white people an explanation on this matter. If a negro complains that the "white" section of our American flag offends his sensitive soul, shall we haul down the flag? How far shall the white people be expected to go in appeasing the whims of the African race?

Yours truly,
Mothers League of Central High
Margaret C. Jackson, president

Chapter Twelve

PERSONAL THREATS
AND BOMB SCARES

AN IMPORTANT, and perhaps the most vicious, phase of the segregationist campaign to close Central High School was harassment of school officials with anonymous telephone calls, often in the middle of the night. Members of the School Board and members of the high school staff all were victims of these tactics over a period of many weeks, but I suppose I was the target more than anyone else.

It was obvious soon after federal troops were stationed at the high school that the telephone campaign was carefully organized so that it would cause us the greatest possible distress. The telephone at my office and at my home rang with great regularity throughout the day, and in the evening the calls were scheduled so that there was at least one every half hour without fail. Sometimes this schedule was continued until three or four o'clock in the morning.

My family, of course, suffered the consequences as much as I did and my wife probably took the worst of it. But she was determined not to be intimidated by threats or taunts and she showed great courage throughout a time of really tremendous tension. Our younger daughter was a senior in high school. She was eligible to attend the nonintegrated Hall High School, a new building in the area where we lived. But she was a cheer leader at Central High School and she insisted that she wanted to return there for her senior year—and she did, regardless of anonymous threats.

Most of the threats were made over the telephone and usually the caller spoke briefly and hung up. Typical remarks—omitting the profanity—were:

"Ain't you proud of what you're doing to the white race?"

"Traitor!"

"Hello, you nigger-loving s.o.b."

"How'd you like some dynamite under your house?"

"We're out to get you!"

There were, too, callers who just hissed or gave a raspberry cheer or swore at me and hung up. Others tried to speak like a Negro until they were sure they had my attention—and then they just cursed me. Some callers wanted to argue with me and would have gone on for hours if I hadn't hung up.

When the phone rang in the middle of the night, my wife often protested that I was asleep. The caller usually tried to make her arouse me anyway. "I can't sleep because of what he's doing," one woman caller said at two o'clock one morning, "so why should he?"

Another woman called my wife one afternoon and asked many questions about where she and I were born and where we were educated.

"Why are you so interested?" my wife asked.

"I had a man come to my door and tell me that Virgil Blossom is a card-carrying Communist and that he could prove it," she replied. "I wanted to check up."

Once my mother was at our house and answered the telephone.

The caller asked for me and my mother said she didn't know where I was. "Well," the caller said, "tell him I've just made up my mind that if I ever lay eyes on him I'll shoot him."

Anonymous callers frequently pretended they were well-known NAACP officials and invited us to dinner or to some other social occasion, and boys often called my daughter to tell her that her father was "a nigger lover." As the weeks went by, such vicious harassment could not fail to have some effect on all of us. One afternoon my secretary called my wife and said: "Mrs. Blossom, I hate to tell you this but after I talked to the FBI agent he said I must call you. You know that several days ago Mr. Blossom got a letter from Jacksonville, Florida, saying that the writer was leaving immediately for Little Rock and was going to 'get' him. Well, this afternoon a man with a very pleasant voice telephoned and said: 'Did you know that at seven-thirty tomorrow morning Virgil Blossom will be shot?' The FBI agent said I must tell you."

My wife tried not to let the threat bother her, but I observed that at seven-thirty the next morning she was peeping out the window to see if there were any strangers nearby, and I knew that the continual threats were leaving their mark.

One afternoon two men came to the door and said they were state termite inspectors and wanted to inspect the basement. My wife let them in and they were there about an hour. After they had left, the telephone rang and a man's voice said:

"How'd you like a couple of sticks of dynamite under your house?"

When I got home that evening, she told me about the call and we tried to laugh it off. Then she remembered the two "inspectors" who had been under the house. They had not shown her any credentials and we could not help being seriously alarmed. I called the pest control company and asked them to check on whether any legitimate state inspectors had been sent to our house, and also to send men out to check the house. They called back to say they couldn't find that any inspector had been sent.

This sounded so bad that about eight-thirty my wife and daughter went over to a neighbor's. An hour later, the company called again and said they had finally located the inspectors, and everything was all right, except for our shaken nerves.

There were two occasions—that I know about—on which the threats were real. Following the warning from Jacksonville, the police assigned two detectives to accompany me for a few days. One day I had to visit the federal building at the time of the injunction hearing against Governor Faubus. Returning to my office parking lot, the detectives' automobile fell behind. As I parked my car, two men jumped out of an automobile at the curb and started for me. Before they reached me, the detectives' car pulled into the parking lot and, seeing it, the men ran back to their car and drove away so quickly the officers could not catch them.

On another occasion, I was driving home late in the evening along one of the principal streets. As I approached my house, a shot fired by a concealed sniper struck the heavy edge of the door of my car where it could not penetrate the metal, but did make a half-inch-deep dent. FBI experts told me later that it was a low-calibre bullet, but they had little idea of what kind of gun was used. For obvious reasons, we kept these incidents secret and, in fact, they have never been told until this was written.

I might add here that numerous attempts were made during the year to force the ouster of school authorities and city officials who had angered segregationists by trying to obey the law. At one time, petitions were circulated calling on the School Board to fire me. This effort did not get far but, after the federal troops arrived, members of the School Board and Police Chief Potts also were targets of ouster petitions and frequent denunciations by segregationists.

In February, the Capital Citizens' Council's attorney, Amis Guthridge, consulted with Prosecuting Attorney Frank Holt with a view to charging me and members of the School Board with malfeasance and nonfeasance. Several Central High School students, who had been suspended for interracial agitation, accompanied Guthridge when he went to see Holt. The attorney asked the prosecutor to seek criminal warrants for my arrest and for the arrest of certain Board members.

If Holt would file informations in circuit court charging school authorities with malfeasance, Guthridge said, we would automatically be removed from office and a county judge would have the power to name our successors until the case was heard. After a two-hour conference, Holt announced that there was insufficient evidence to comply with the request.

"With his [Holt's] connections, we were wasting our time," Guthridge said later. "I disagree with Mr. Holt in his analysis of the situation but the decision came out exactly as I had expected it." He added that Holt had been a deputy prosecutor under former prosecutor Edwin E. Dunaway, who was president of the Urban League of Greater Little Rock.

The Rev. Wesley Pruden, president of the Capital Citizens' Council, frequently predicted that I would be fired. "The temple is going to fall in soon on Virgil Blossom," he said in a public speech in March, 1958. "Blossom's days as superintendent are numbered."

II

In addition to nuisance telephone calls, there were repeated anonymous threats that the high school would be bombed, or tips that a bomb had been planted in the school. These were a part of the campaign to force closure of the integrated school, and in a period of several months we received at least forty-three such bomb-scare telephone calls. In general, they followed a set pattern. The anonymous call would first be made to one of the newspapers or radio stations or to all of them, presumably to be sure there would be maximum publicity and that parents would worry about sending their children to the school. Then the anonymous caller would get in touch with the police or one of the school officials and repeat the threat or the "tip" that a bomb had been planted. On some days during October and November we had several such calls on one day and once we had five.

To explain how these threats were handled I must go back to May of 1957, when the School Board was confident that its integration plan would be accepted, but when segregationist opposition was just beginning to emerge in an important way. On that occasion, I was in a School Board meeting when someone told me I was wanted on the telephone. It was a reporter from one of the newspapers.

"We've just received a couple of anonymous calls that a bomb has been planted in Central High," he said. "The callers said it was a protest against integration."

The public participation in the School Board meeting ended shortly afterward and I asked the Board members to remain. When I told them of the bomb threat, one of the members said: "I think you should get on the radio and tell the students there won't be any school tomorrow. Then we can search the building."

Another member expressed doubt as to that course. "If we are intimidated by this threat and close down the school even for a day," he said, "we will put ourselves at the mercy of the extremists. All they will have to do to keep the school closed is to start a new bomb scare every day or so."

I agreed that it might not be necessary to close the school and suggested that, with the aid of the police, we organize a search party that night. The Board finally decided that would be best, and they gave me the responsibility for making the search and then deciding whether to close the school the next day.

I secured the aid of the police—they were tirelessly co-operative throughout the following months—and we searched the school building that night from basement to rooftop. It took about four hours and we didn't find any bombs. As a result, I decided the call was a hoax and school was not interrupted.

But fear of a bomb was a potent weapon in the hands of extremists, and in October, after the Army was on the job, the anonymous "tips" began coming again to the newspapers, police and school authorities. The Board continued to leave in my hands any decision on closing the school, and nobody had to remind me that it was a grave responsibility. My daughter was among the two thousand children in the building. So was the son of Principal Matthews.

Of course, we knew that most of the bomb scares were false and believed that some of them were initiated by students as a "prank." But we also knew we could never take a chance, and we made a search after every threat. This was not only a tremendous headache for the police and the school staff, but it was very expensive because we finally had to hire extra night guards and organize teams of searchers, who became expert at the job. The magnitude of the task was perhaps best indicated by the testimony at a later court hearing of O. W. Romine, the director of School Plant Services, who had been forced to increase the number of night watchmen from one to six at a cost of $195 each per month.

Q. Were you aware of any of the searches . . . as a result of bomb threats?

A. I organized search parties on forty-three different occasions.

Q. Explain just what you did to cope with that problem.

A. I organized a search crew of ten men who were employes of the school district when we got a bomb threat or had occasion to search the building. It took us about six hours with ten men. . . . It was quite an undertaking. You keep in mind there's 2,600 student lockers in the building. There were 1,900 of them in use. Of the 1,900 practically all had combination locks on. We were supplied with [a master list of] the combinations. We would take the serial number from the lock and work the combination, open the locker and search it.

Q. Some of the lockers were . . . not in use. Did you search those?

A. Yes, sir. [and] there is a panel in the base of the lockers. We had to remove that panel (with a screwdriver) and search the recess area in the base of the lockers . . . In order to save time we [later] secured the doors with metal links on the empty lockers. We found they were being removed and prized off, and later [we] used a bolt and bolted the door securely with the threads on it battered so it could not be removed. That saved us the trouble of searching some 600 vacant lockers.

Q. Could you always get into the [occupied] lockers?

A. In many cases we found that students would bring in a foreign combination lock, of which we did not have the combination. We cut the lock off. . . . The children were paid for the locks, part of them. . . . On one occasion I recall seeing a bushel basket full of the locks that had been cut off. . . . They cost us $1.25 per each.

Q. These searching crews . . . did you pay them for that service?

A. We did, at the rate of $1.50 an hour.

Not all of the bomb "tips" were hoaxes. One night I was called from home late in the evening during a search of the school and helped Gene Smith, who had become Police Chief, remove a home-made bomb from one of the lockers. It was a long, thin bottle filled with gunpowder and shot and with a fuse about eighteen inches long. The fuse had been lighted, apparently just after school was dismissed for the day, but the fire had gone out before it reached the bomb. On two other occasions we found similar home-made bombs that had not been lighted so far as we could tell, and one morning while school was in session we found two sticks of dynamite, but with no caps or detonator attached. These presumably were planted to make the authorities take the bomb-scare telephone calls seriously, as we did. We particularly feared that a bomb might wreck the furnace and force closing of the school and we guarded the furnace room twenty-four hours a day.

After a number of expensive bomb searches, I attempted to

arrange with police and telephone company officials to trace the next anonymous call that came to the principal's office at Central High School. This proved very difficult to do, but with the co-operation of the telephone company top officials we finally set up a complicated system of detection. It required us to have a special routing for calls to the school and it was necessary for the police to remain on the alert to speed to the source of the call. After secretly making all the arrangements and after making sure that only a very few top company and police officials knew of our plan, we decided to put the system into operation on a Monday morning. We didn't, however, because on Sunday evening my telephone rang and a voice said: "Tell Mr. Blossom not to bother about trying to trace telephone calls. We know all the details of the system he has set up."

Chapter Thirteen

SCHOOL MUST KEEP
UNDER TENSION

I SAID EARLIER that I believed disorders inside Central High School were due more to outside influences than to the initiative of fewer than fifty students who formed a nucleus of resistance to integration. Some of the outside influence was simply the shift of public opinion against integration as a result of federal intervention. The organized segregationist campaign, however, did a great deal to bring about and to harden that change of community attitude and it had a very definite effect on the attitude of students at the high school.

The big majority of the children continued to be tolerant and to show respect for the law, but they also quickly recognized the temper of their elders and they trimmed their own sails to the wind. They no longer made many special efforts to be friendly toward the Negro students, such as occasionally inviting them to sit at their tables in the cafeteria. They adopted a passive rather than a helpful attitude. They kept their opinions to themselves instead of telling reporters or radio interviewers they were not opposed to integration.

After one school leader who had been friendly toward the Negro students was pushed against a wall by several white boys, and after others had received threatening telephone calls, the students were very careful about expressing their opinions, and most of them remained silent about integration even when talking with classmates. They maintained their dignity and their right to think as they pleased, but, as community feeling hardened, they were deprived in effect of their freedom of speech.

In addition, the active segregation-minded students appeared to come more and more under the influence of outsiders during the last three months of 1957. J. O. Powell, vice-principal for boys at Central High School, later testified in a court hearing that there were perhaps a hundred students involved in one way or another in disturbances in the school, but that only five to ten boys were "leaders of the opposition to integration."

"They were leaders or the tools of outside adult leadership," he added. "Either they were used by agitators outside—adult groups outside the schools—or they were simply jumping on the fun wagon and repeating themselves for the variety of it."

"How do you account for the attitude of the students who have created these incidents?" he was asked.

"I think that attitude germinates from outside adult groups," Powell replied.

"If you removed the so-called ring leaders, that . . . would not solve all the other integration problems involved, would it? It wouldn't do anything in helping you solve any outside influence on those students or any people over whom you have no right to attempt to control, would it?"

"No, sir."

"And it is your opinion that those outside influences have tremendously influenced the activities of Central High School?"

"Yes, sir."

I might mention here that my wife and I spent a good deal of time worrying about the effect of all this on our daughter, who was in the senior class. She went about her work as usual, which was with a great deal of energy, and she was active in school affairs. We often waited with considerable trepidation when she appeared in some public activity—she was one of the school cheer leaders at football games, for example—in fear that students or others might make her the target of jeers or abusive remarks merely because she was my daughter.

I guess some of her friends were a bit worried, too, because at one time several members of the football team secretly appointed themselves as a committee to watch over her. She didn't know it at the time, nor did I, but these boys got a schedule of her classes and one of them was always on hand when she went from one class to another—just in case anybody made any remarks to her.

But they need not have worried, nor need we have worried. She never had a moment's serious trouble.

II

Within a week after the Army had taken over, disturbances inside Central High School were creating problems almost every day for teachers and guards. Few of these were of a really serious nature, and many incidents between students might have been regarded as no more than normal if it had not been for the racial issue. But, under the circumstances, almost any minor brush between white and Negro students became a major incident, particularly in the eyes of newspaper reporters, who were not permitted inside but gathered every day, usually flanked by photographers, across the street. As a result, any news that came from inside the school was good for a newspaper headline, especially if it indicated racial friction.

There certainly was friction, a large part of it originating with members of the sophomore class. During the previous year the staff had put special emphasis on schooling senior high school students in citizenship and responsibility for law obedience. Unfortunately, such training had not been given similar emphasis in the junior high school. As a result, in the fall of 1957 the sophomores, who were newcomers to the senior high school, were less well prepared to adjust themselves to integration than were the members of the junior and senior classes. Furthermore, teachers did not know potential troublemakers in the sophomore class as well as they knew those in upper classes.

Some students refused to participate in the customary morning ceremony of pledging allegiance to the government of the United States, saying they would not take part as long as federal soldiers "occupied" the school building. Others created disturbances in the corridors when they were least likely to be observed or in the cafeteria, where food spilled on a Negro student could be blamed on an "accident." I do not wish to name any of the children involved in these incidents. They were, generally speaking, immature and under the influence of others, and in most cases they either left the school voluntarily or by order of the School Board—or they changed their attitude and became well-behaved before the end of the year. But I cannot avoid saying that all the Negro students except one behaved well—almost stoically—under severe provocation. They had, of course, been specially selected, they had been carefully briefed by their parents, they were counseled by teachers to avoid retaliation and they were serving a cause. The one exception was a girl. She was bright and high-strung and quick-tempered and perhaps not as mature as the others. In any event, she had difficulty in adjusting to the extremely difficult situation in which she was placed. She showed her resentment when harassed by white students and they, in turn, made her a special target for their jibes.

After preliminary gestures of hostility, a few white students became bolder in their abuse of the Negroes in October. Two Negro girl students were shoved around in a corridor, verbally abused and blocked from their classroom door by several white boys. Later, one of the girls was struck by small pebbles and hard candies as she walked along a crowded corridor. Another was kicked by a boy as she went to her seat in the assembly. Several boys made a practice of following one Negro girl in the corridors and calling her vulgar names in low voices. Once the girl turned on them and replied in similar language.

On several occasions, the participants in these incidents ended up in the principal's office, where Matthews or his assistant, Elizabeth Huckaby, lectured them and counseled the Negro students not to reply to such harassment in the hope it would die out. But it did not die out. After several brushes, a white boy and a Negro boy got into a scuffle and the Negro boy was knocked down. The white boy was suspended.

"It was simply a case of one boy hitting another without provocation," Principal Matthews said later. "Suspension in such cases is automatic."

The *State Press*, a Negro newspaper, reporting the incident in exaggerated terms, speculated as to whether General Walker was "bowing to local pressure" by failing to provide sufficient protection inside the school building. Mrs. Daisy Bates came to the school to complain about conditions. She was quoted by the Associated Press as saying that the Negro children "are being bullied and harassed to try to force them to leave. But they're not going to give in."

Mrs. Jackson, of the Mothers League, said that "there is great resentment against the Negroes inside the school. The white children are determined to get them out of there. There will be bloodshed if all the troops are taken away."

The *Arkansas Gazette* had six reporters interview Central High School students and teachers late in November and published the following summarized conclusions:

A white girl sits down for lunch with a Negro student in the Central High School cafeteria and finds herself ostracized by other students. She doesn't do it again.

A Negro student violates an unwritten class rule not to study oral assignments and comes up with the right answers. His classmates feel he is "smarting off."

The literary-minded give up the practice of writing vulgarisms on the restroom walls, start scribbling a different kind of inscription: "Nigger go home."

A Negro girl jostles a white girl in the hall and the white girl spits on her. A teacher sees this and looks away.

An English class has a spelling match and one team captain chooses a Negro student first. . . .

A white boy doesn't "give a damn" about Negroes in the school, says, "I don't care if they stay or go." He's interested only in getting a scholarship.

Practically all of the students, regardless of their feelings about integration, are convinced of one thing: Classwork is tougher this year than ever before. . . .

That is Central High School after 12 weeks. Not entirely calm, by any means, but not in turmoil either.

The evidence, from interviews with teachers and students, is that Central has learned to live with tension but nobody knows what's ahead. There is widespread talk of gangs being formed, dedicated to making trouble for the Negroes when the troops leave.

They make as much trouble for the Negroes now as they can get away with. But most of the time the nine Negro students study and move about in almost total isolation from their 2,000 white classmates because the whites who once tried to befriend them have been intimidated, either by social ostracism or open threats. . . .

There is a feeling among some faculty members that the incidents involving the Negro students have been played out of all perspective. Some, they feel, are the type of incidents that have nothing to do with integration but are the result of frictions that are natural to teen-agers. . . .

During the period of October and November guards were assigned to accompany the Negro students from one class to another in order to prevent them from being molested.

One Negro girl irritated her classmates because she sometimes laughed and motioned to her guard imperiously when she came out of a classroom, drawling: "Come on, guard. Now I'm going to another class." Again, she remarked as she passed a guard on the stairway: "I could do a better job than that!" Then, in mid-December, a Negro girl went to the cafeteria at noon one day and started to carry a bowl of chili to a table. En route, a couple of chairs were shoved into her path and she became so angry that she threw her tray on the head of a white boy sitting nearby, splashing chili over several students.

Actually, I was later convinced that the chair shoving was entirely accidental. Both boys involved said that they had no resentment against the Negro students and that they had not intended to block her path. Nevertheless, the damage was done, and the school authorities had to take some action. The principal, with my agreement, suspended the Negro girl for two weeks.

III

In mid-December, the segregationist activity seemed to be stepped up in an effort to take advantage of troubles inside the school. For example, the Capital Citizens' Council distributed a circular through the mails charging that there was

a vicious fear campaign in process at Central High School, whereby the white children are being told that at any time a white child has trouble with a Negro student the white student must face Daisy Bates and be cross-examined by her.

Daisy Bates was allowed to cross-examine a number of white students recently following a kick-fight between a white girl and a Negro girl. Because the white girl would not answer Daisy Bates' questions, Mr. Matthews gave the white girl two weeks in the detention hall. Who is running Central High School? Blossom or Bates—or both!

This account was fabricated out of an instance when the state president of the NAACP had discussed with Matthews a disturbance that had occurred at the school. She never cross-examined white students.

At about the same time Matthews received a letter from Mrs. Jackson saying that the Mothers League was positively convinced that conditions at Central High School have reached a disgraceful low.

We are protesting with every impulse and energy of our soul the way you are conducting yourself and the affairs of the school. The common decencies of one white person to another are being outraged —to say nothing of the respect a white child has a right to expect of a white school official. To be hated by a child is certainly no compliment to a grownup.

Specifically, we of the Mothers' League of Central High resent and protest the following outrages:

That you have surrendered completely to the Virgil Blossom forces and are working feverishly and without conscience to implement the Blossom Plan—a plan so obnoxious to both parents and children of Little Rock that the armed might of the United States Army is necessary to give the plan even the semblance of success.

We resent and protest the obvious fact that your sympathies and love are altogether on the side of the negroes. In every incident of violence between a white and negro student, you suspend, discipline or otherwise humiliate the white child and exonerate the negro. Many white students, but not one negro student has been suspended.

Recently, when a negro girl student cursed a white girl student and the incident was reported to you, you were reported as saying to the white girl that she would have to learn how negroes talked and adjust to it as best she could. This we resent and protest. . . .

We have information that yesterday, December 12, a negro girl kicked a white boy. The white boy struck the negro girl. The negro girl was exonerated. The white boy was disciplined. This we resent and protest.

We resent your giving Daisy Bates free and happy access to the school building to confer with you personally and frequently while white parents are denied the privilege. Daisy Bates is not a paid employee of the school (we hope) and has no children in the school.

From numerous and valid sources there comes information that you have given to Daisy Bates the right of cross examination of our children at Central High School when fights or trouble break out between the

Negro and white students. Mr. Matthews, this is a disgraceful betrayal of the trust that the white parents have placed in you. They have entrusted their children to you and you turn them over to a Negro woman who is constantly in company with known communists. Mr. Matthews, if you deny this we will prove it. On more than one occasion you have done this.

We further resent the iron-clad censorship you have clapped on our High School. In this crucial and tragic period not even the parents are permitted to know all that is happening to their children at school.

We resent the fear campaign you have instigated among our children at Central High School. An almost prisonlike fear and mental paralysis has come on the children, since they have been told that anytime a child crosses one of Daisy Bates' children that the white child will have to give an account to Daisy Bates personally.

A copy of this letter is being mailed to Virgil Blossom and also to the School Board. This is our first step toward correcting the insufferable outrages the white parents and their children are suffering at the hands of a negro dominated school administration.

The letter was a complete misrepresentation of what had happened, but it was given wide publicity.

We had hoped that disciplinary action such as the suspension of some students would end the incidents in the school, but after the Christmas vacation things became worse instead of better—thanks in part, at least, to the increased agitation of segregationist organizations, which hoped to rid the school of Negroes at midterm. A white boy called a Negro girl a "nigger-looking bitch" and refused to obey the order of a guard to report to the principal's office. A white boy kicked a Negro girl as she was leaving school.

A white student was suspended after brushing against or shoving a Negro girl in a corridor. The white girl claimed that the Negro girl "started to hit me" but witnesses did not support her version. The parents of a Negro girl attempted to get a warrant against a white boy they said had kicked their daughter, but the Pulaski County prosecutor declined to bring charges. The boy said that previously he had been sitting in a class with his feet in the aisle when the girl came along and said: "Move your feet, white boy." The boy said he didn't move and that the girl struck him on the leg and later called him "white trash." He said he had then received several threatening telephone calls which he believed came from Negroes who "threatened to kill us all—me and my Mom and Dad."

At this time we were having bomb-scare telephone calls every day or so and the staff was under great pressure. So were the students. For several days, a group of boys and girls followed one of the Negro girls in the corridors and whispered at her: "Nigger-nigger." Finally, the girl stopped suddenly in a corridor while being closely followed and one of the white girls ran into her. It was not easy to determine just what happened after that, but, from the statements of those involved and witnesses, we got the general picture.

The white girl used vulgar language and concluded by saying: "You think you're smart, don't you? If you stop like that again, I'll kick you like that boy did!"

The Negro girl then moved on to her classroom, followed by the white girl, who continued to make provocative remarks. After the Negro girl had gone into her classroom the white girl stood in the doorway, still talking.

"Will you please stop talking to me, white trash?" the Negro girl finally said.

The white girl flung her purse and hit the Negro girl in the head. The Negro girl picked up the purse and threw it back at the other girl's feet. By that time, one of the guards had come up and said to both girls: "All right, let's go to the office."

Mrs. Huckaby talked to the two girls and they agreed, in part, as to what had happened. The white girl said she threw the purse because she had been called a name. The Negro girl said she had been repeatedly followed and called names by the white girl and several others. Mrs. Huckaby took both girls to the principal's office and Matthews reviewed the case and told them they were both wrong and should admit it and agree to keep out of each other's way in the future. The Negro girl agreed and was sent on to her class, but the white girl said only: "I don't know."

Mrs. Huckaby suggested she might want to go home and talk to her parents. She agreed and telephoned her home, but then asked Mrs. Huckaby to talk to her mother. The girl's father later came to the school and said he believed it would be best if the girl withdrew and went to school elsewhere. Mrs. Huckaby informed me that the father was not critical of the school authorities but merely of the situation and he predicted that eventually some child would be injured. The girl collected her gym clothes and left with her father shortly after ten o'clock.

The news of her withdrawal apparently spread quickly to other students and some of them blamed the Negro girl. Just after noon, Mrs. Huckaby found the Negro girl standing outside her office, trembling and sobbing.

"Can I go home?" she asked.

"Come inside and tell me why," Mrs. Huckaby replied.

"Because I can't keep from crying," she said. She then went into the office with Mrs. Huckaby and explained that a group of girls in her glee club class had stood behind her and "said things to me." They apparently accused her of having the white girl "put out of school"—which was not true, of course—and said they were going to "report" her, apparently to segregationist leaders inside or outside the school. After Mrs. Huckaby had talked to her, the girl seemed to be feeling better and went to the cafeteria for lunch.

Ten minutes later she came running back up the stairs, crying and followed by a guard. Not far behind them was a large group of students, mostly boys, making a lot of noise. Mrs. Huckaby took her into the office and closed the door. The back of the girl's dress was badly stained with soup. She was told to change her clothes and the school nurse examined her to be sure she had not been burned.

"What happened?" Mrs. Huckaby asked.

"I don't know," the girl replied.

Later, teachers who had been in the cafeteria said that a white boy had walked up behind her and thrown a bowl of soup on her. A teacher had grabbed the boy and called a guard, who took him to Mrs. Huckaby's office.

When the guard brought the boy to the office the crowd of students in the hall created a disturbance. A girl screamed wildly and other girls scrambled for the telephone booths to call their parents. Mrs. Huckaby tried without much success to order the fifty or sixty students milling about in the hall to go to their classrooms. Finally, she told one of the staff to ring the bell, although it was five minutes early. The hall was cleared slowly. The Negro girl called her mother, who came to the school and took her home.

After Matthews had fully investigated the incident, the boy who had thrown the soup was suspended. We were frankly reluctant to expell the Negro girl, not so much because of the effect on her as because we feared that if she were expelled the school troublemakers would then concentrate on some or all of the other Negro students and make their lives miserable. However, the girl had not been able to adjust and, so far as we could see, there was little hope that further serious trouble could be avoided if she returned to the school. Furthermore, after several warnings and after her promises not to exchange insults with other students, she had used vulgar language to her tormentors.

"I have suspended your daughter," I wrote to her parents, "for two weeks. I am further recommending to the Little Rock Board of Education that this suspension be extended through the 1957-58 school year. I am making this recommendation . . . because it is my best judgment that [she] has shown an inability to adjust to a difficult situation. After a careful review of the situation, I feel that this action is best for the school and for your daughter."

The School Board confirmed my decision in the case, but the girl's parents protested and wrote to the Board asking that she be reinstated. "We feel that this charge is unfair," their letter said, "when it is considered the type of treatment she was expected to adjust to. We believe the attacks have been planned and were intended to occur daily. This belief is substantiated by students attending the school. . . . These incidents are not casual ones, but apparently premeditated with the intent to cause an incident whereby [she] would be expelled."

"They throw rocks at you, they spill ink on you—and we just have to be little lambs and take it," the Negro girl said later. "The boys can't really hurt you but the girls know they can—and they're vicious."

The Board, however, declined to reinstate her.

IV

Our fears that the expulsion would work a hardship on the other Negro students were immediately confirmed. The next morning Matthews discovered that several students were passing out printed cards to everybody who would take them. The cards said:

ONE DOWN AND
EIGHT TO GO!

That evening, incidentally, while I was sitting in a restaurant, one of these cards was dropped on my table by someone passing, but I failed to recognize the man who did it.

One of those who passed out the cards at school was a white girl who was intelligent and had marked qualities of leadership, but who was obviously under strong outside influence by segregationists whom we never definitely identified. She had been somewhat involved in various incidents at the school, but always managed to avoid anything that would cause her to be suspended. She made no secret of her opposition to integration, however. She wore "Remember Little Rock" badges and on several occasions had been suspected of shoving or otherwise harassing Negro girl students in the corridors. A favorite trick of some of the girls was to follow the Negro students closely and step on their heels as they walked through the halls, something that could always be passed off as accidental if necessary.

This girl had been punished at various times for her activities, particularly for absences from school when her mother didn't know where she had gone. A teacher once told me the girl had boasted that she had "sat across the desk" from the Governor and talked to him and that she had plenty of segregationist business outside of school hours. She also charged on one occasion that a Negro boy had made "familiar" remarks and winked at her, but investigation provided not the slightest grounds for the accusation. When she was called upon in English class to give a motion picture review, she delivered a segregationist propaganda talk on the movie *Belle Starr*. On another occasion, she made a quick change of clothes with another white girl in an effort to prevent a guard from identifying the latter as one who had verbally abused a Negro student.

After a prolonged period of such activities, the girl finally was suspended because she was "unable to conform to the standards of conduct requisite for high school pupils." The faculty's impression that she was being guided by adults outside the school was not lessened by the fact that segregationist leaders, including the Reverend Wesley Pruden and Amis Guthridge, immediately launched a protest campaign to have her reinstated.

An advertisment was run in the newspapers by the Freedom Fund for Little Rock announcing that the girl—"expelled from Central High School!"—would appear on a television show. She "will be interviewed by prominent Little Rock Citizens and will reveal the shocking conditions existing in Central High School," the announcement said. "You will be horrified at the conditions which heretofor have been wrapped in a military-like censorship."

The television interview—a repetition of the Mothers League charges—and the protest campaign stirred up a great deal of public feeling, and the controversy was intensified when the girl's parents filed a suit in Pulaski Circuit Court demanding her readmission. Our feeling at the time was that a court order to reinstate the girl would practically wreck discipline at Central High School.

Fortunately, a lawyer who was a friend of the girl's family suggested an out-of-court compromise. The girl wrote a letter to the Board promising to conform to the rules of the school if she were reinstated. The Board obviously was in a difficult position and common sense dictated acceptance of the offer in the interest of all. After the girl's return to classes, she lived up to her promise in every way and her behavior was exemplary for the remainder of the year.

V

There were many incidents during the school year that I have not mentioned because, for the most part, they would be repetitious. I think I can best sum up our experience by saying that during the year 1957-58 the students and staff of Central High School were under very great tension most of the time and that it was not possible to carry on normal educational processes. Later, during court proceedings, an attorney asked Mrs. Huckaby whether the tension and the constant threat of violence had any effect on the success or failure of the school program.

It certainly did [she replied]. There was hardly a day some teacher did not come to me . . . a-tremble. They had observed for the first time in their lives the violence of one person toward another human being, and it was tremendously upsetting. . . . I would lie awake at night wondering what I could do. . . . I had no social life at all because on weekends I was too tired. . . . I would go to the country. . . . and just sit and usually by noon Sunday I would begin to revive enough to face the next week.

Another witness, J. O. Powell, vice-principal for boys, also testified as to his experiences during the year:

Q. . . . what can you tell the Court of the general disciplinary problems that you had . . . ?

A. I would say I have spent at least twenty per cent more of my time on disciplinary problems during the current year than I have previously.

Q. Mr. Powell, could you tell us, just on a more or less typical day, the sort of thing you had to deal with . . . ?

A. Let's say I arrive at the school at seven-thirty . . . Between seven-thirty and seven-forty, the switchboard gets a bomb call. These . . . are routed through me . . . to the military, to the superintendent's office, to the city police and to the FBI and CID and other interested agencies. Then [there would be] following through with the supervision of the bomb search. . . . Then, say at eight-thirty, a guard or teacher may bring a colored or white student to the office for having been involved in an incident. It takes twenty minutes to reduce those statements with a guard and the student to writing and to make a record. If we follow that up with a conference with the principal that runs into approximately another thirty or forty minutes. Meanwhile, a rumor gets started and people go to the telephone and make calls to the press or various other parties. [Then] the city police or the FBI may come to the office for detailed reports of what went on from all persons concerned. That involves time. Around nine o'clock, let's say, a boy calls the school requesting we send word to a girl recently reinstated from suspension that he would like to speak to her. . . . The telephone operator says that the call is from a colored boy . . . so that stirs things up. That gets the switchboard operator excited and it certainly is a different type of harassment. . . .

And, on a rough day, I may be able to get in a full hour of normal routine school work.

O. W. Romine, the director of the School Plant Services, also testified that at least thirty fires were started by students in lockers and wastebaskets and that there were many instances of vandalism by students opposed to integration:

Q. Tell us some of the particular problems of maintenance. . . .

A. We had quite a problem coping with breakage and damage occurring in the restrooms. . . . The walls and even the ceiling and fixtures were mutilated. All types of obscene writing and drawing occurred on the walls. . . . Where they cut into the plaster above the wainscoating we would have to re-plaster the wall and then re-paint it.

Q. Would it be fair to say this problem was many, many times over what it had ever been before?

A. Yes.

Q. Do you attribute that to the integration problem?

A. I would say it was a direct result. . . . I am basing that on the nature of the writings on the walls and obscene pictures. . . . It started in September and continued throughout the year. . . . It was necessary to remove the steam radiators in some of the rest rooms.

Q. Will you explain why?

A. These were floor radiators and the fact that students urinated on those radiators when they were hot caused fumes to go through the entire building.

Q. Did that create quite a stench?

A. It did.

The strain on the staff was not due entirely to the activities of pupils. Throughout this period, state officials and legislative committees were actively concerned with enforcement of the state's segregation laws or preparing for new legislation. Members of the state police frequently requested interviews with teachers at Central High School in regard to integration, the behavior of pupils and the effect on the educational program. Such interviews were on a voluntary basis but, after a few weeks, members of the staff complained to me that the reports made by the police officers did not accurately represent what had been said during the interviews. The teachers, all of whom tried to do a good job regardless of their personal views on integration, felt that the police reports were being slanted to favor the segregationist viewpoint.

Since the staff did not wish to be put in a false position of refusing to co-operate by ceasing to talk to the police, I suggested that we transcribe the interviews so there could be no misunderstanding of what was said. I then hired a court reporter and instructed him to be present whenever the teachers were questioned. Thereafter, the state police ceased interviewing members of the school staff.

VI

I believe that, after reciting all of these difficulties during the school year, I may take this opportunity to quote from an article by John N. Popham in the *New York Times,* an article which, as you will understand, expressed some of my own feelings. The writer said that a consensus of the people of Little Rock would sound like this:

If ever a group was stuck out in left field, it is our school superintendent Virgil T. Blossom and the six members of the School Board. They have complied with desegregation orders of the federal judiciary . . . [but] there isn't any local leadership to bolster the school officials. Congress hasn't done anything . . . our governor has opposed integration . . . our state legislature has adopted laws and resolutions to block integration . . . and even a state court at one point ruled against integration in Little Rock at this time. . . . The school officials are harassed, buffeted and badgered day and night by the extremists. . . . They have no supporting leadership to explain and define their position, even to boost their morale. True, there are a lot of people here who are proud of the school officials and their respect for judicial processes. The school officials have been getting heartening messages from all over the state. [But] . . . it certainly seems evident that the role of the law-abiding school official warrants a lot of sympathetic study!

I suppose at times the School Board and the Central High School staff and I became depressed by what was happening, and I know we appreciated the sympathetic and encouraging letters—there were many of them—that came to us and to the editors of the Little Rock newspapers, particularly those from Southerners.

But I hope we didn't ever feel sorry for ourselves. We had a difficult and often nerve-racking job to do but I know that most of us were determined to do it as honestly and as fairly as we possibly could. We were not perfect and I have no doubt that we made mistakes. I don't believe, however, that either the Board or the school staff of one hundred shirked their duty to the children in their charge or their duty as citizens of the United States.

It became obvious to me later that, despite all of the publicity attending the Little Rock integration controversy, there was considerable confusion in the minds of the American people as to details of what had happened. When I attended a meeting of the American Association of School Administrators in St. Louis, I talked with many prominent educators. Most of them were both interested and sympathetic when we discussed the Little Rock integration problem but a few were somewhat critical of the expulsion of the Negro girl from Central High School, feeling that the Board had made a serious psychological mistake.

But to them I replied, "During the school year we suspended approximately one hundred white students and expelled four while twenty-five others—including some of the leading troublemakers—withdrew from school. And only one Negro student was expelled."

It turned out that they had no idea that so many white students had been disciplined and I felt that they changed their minds when they had the complete story.

Federal troops remained at Central High throughout the school year. In the spring, the disturbances at Central High School decreased but we faced a final crisis when the time came for commencement exercises late in May, 1958. At that time, segregationists became active again, hinting that there would be trouble if a Negro was publicly graduated. The Negro students had all done well during the school year and one of them, Ernest Green, was eligible to be graduated with the senior class.

There were several suggestions to the School Board that Ernest should not be graduated, or that he should receive his diploma privately instead of at the usual ceremonies in the athletic stadium. The School Board refused to knuckle under to such proposals and it also decided that it was not going to have a military-dominated commencement. And we didn't. We gave every student the same number of tickets—eight—for guests at the ceremonies and, with the aid of city police, we admitted only ticket holders. Eighty National Guardsmen remained out of sight under the stands.

Some 4,500 spectators, including a few adult Negroes, were in the stadium for the ceremonies, at which a choral reading called "The Story of Arkansas" was presented by some of the seniors. It was written by students and told the story of the state and its folkways, and included this reference to pre-Civil War days:

> Negro slaves to old King Cotton
> Toiled beneath the broiling sun,
> While their masters lived in leisure
> Heeding not impending doom.

The audience remained silent during the reading. They also sat in silence as Ernest Green, the first Negro ever graduated from Central High School, received his diploma.

Chapter Fourteen

THE UGLY AFTERMATH

BY THE SUMMER of 1958, the social and political complexion of Little Rock had undergone a tremendous change. Public opinion, which had reluctantly supported our integration plan in the summer of 1957, had become antagonistic after a year of segregationist agitation and eight months of Army-enforced integration at Central High School. In the state generally, people seemed to have lost their sense of proportion. The integration issue overshadowed everything else.

Governor Faubus, who had once been suspected by the segregationists of being a dangerous liberal, was now the hero of the South's resistance to the Supreme Court's desegregation order.

After vainly trying to evade responsibility for enforcement of the Court's decisions, Faubus had surrendered to the pressure of segregationists from all over the South. When it served his political purposes, he had skillfully confused the issue of law obedience with talk of Jeffersonian democracy and Jacksonian democracy and, reluctantly edging toward the twentieth century, the Civil War conflict over states' rights. And, in the end, he provided the impetus that turned a law-abiding people with excellent race relations into a divided and hate-plagued community

176

where citizens, except for an extremist minority, were afraid to speak their minds.

In the course of this transformation, Little Rock had been presented to the world as a symbol of bigotry and racial prejudice. This unenviable public role was entirely undeserved by the great majority of the people of the city and was humiliating to those rendered helpless by the vicious pressures of politics and prejudice.

There have been some responsible journalists who criticized the press for its role in the Little Rock crisis, contending that reporters intensified the trouble because they were inclined to sensationalize incidents of violence and were not inclined to look deeply into the causes of the problem or to present the case of the intelligent and moderate majority. I am no expert in the field of journalism, but I am sure that there were times when the mere presence of scores of reporters from other cities and from abroad was more of a hindrance than a help to the school authorities.

There were occasions, too, when newsmen inadvertently seemed to be pushing the Governor into a stronger and stronger popular position at home by the very intensity of their search for information. On one nationwide television show, for example, some reporters vigorously pressed Faubus with hostile questions about his defiance of the federal government and also about his humble background but they did it in such a way as to create an erroneous impression that he was an uncouth hillbilly. Nothing could have suited the Governor's purposes better. He was neither uncouth nor a hillbilly, but it gave him the opportunity to play the underdog, the humble man of the people fighting not only the big city reporters but the vast power of the federal government. The role had great appeal for the anti-integrationists and he gained popularity day by day. He also took advantage of strong editorial attacks on him by such magazines as *Time* and *Life*, quoting freely from the editorials and denouncing the "foreign" press for attempting to impose their alien ideas on the South.

Although Faubus usually referred to reporters from outside

Arkansas as representing the "foreign" press, we did have a number of journalists present at various times from other countries, and I received clippings and letters from all over the world commenting on what was happening at Little Rock. According to these reports, there were big headlines about Little Rock "even in the rural areas" of Finland. Photographs and news stories from Little Rock appeared "on the front page of practically every newspaper in Europe," particularly the Communist newspapers, with such headlines as "The Race Haters Strike the Young Negroes Who Assist Nine Black Students to Enter the High School!" At Gilgit, in Azad-Kashmir, a young American mountain climber reported there was "news about the Little Rock trouble on virtually every page" of the newspapers, and people repeatedly asked him whether "the United States really practices democracy as it tells us."

A Brazilian government official visited Little Rock and reported that the situation was not "nearly as bad" as had been reported in the Brazilian press. An Arkansas farmer visiting India commented that the Russian launching of the first earth satellite and the developments at Little Rock had been two serious psychological setbacks for the United States in that country of 370,000,000 dark-skinned people. Events at Little Rock were broadcast by Egyptian radio stations beamed to the Sudan for propaganda purposes, the South African Johannesburg *Star* commented unfavorably despite the rigid segregation laws in that country, the newspapers of Ghana carried the news to darkest Africa, the Moscow newspaper *Pravda* and the Vatican newspaper *L'Osservatore Romano* were agreed for the first time in denunciation of Little Rock.

Communists often falsified reports from Little Rock. "Instigated by the school, children started hunting down the nine Negro children who persisted in courageously defending their right to human dignity," Radio Moscow falsely said in a broadcast picked up by the U. S. Information Agency. "Schoolgirl Elizabeth Eckford was brutally murdered a few days ago."

In Caracas, Venezuela, a mob that endangered Vice President Richard Nixon during his good will tour of South America, shouted: "Little Rock! What about Little Rock?"

In Japan, the newspaper *Asahi* kept the people informed of developments by sending its own reporter to Little Rock. Interest was such that after the reporter had returned to Tokyo he called me by overseas telephone to ask for details of an incident inside the school which had been reported in news agency dispatches. In fact, I was the recipient of countless telephone calls from newspapermen in foreign countries, sometimes as many as a score in one day. Although during one period I held two press conferences a day for as many as eighty reporters, there were also many telephone calls daily from newspapers in American cities—so many I could not even try to answer half of them.

II

After school ended in May of 1958, the School Board had to face the problem of whether it could continue its program of gradual integration at the opening of the next term in September in view of vastly hardened segregationist resistance. The Board considered all of the factors involved in great detail and then instructed its attorneys, A. F. House and Richard C. Butler, to ask the federal court to grant a tactical delay—a "cooling-off" period—of two and one-half years in which to prepare a more favorable climate for integration. The request was heard by Federal District Judge Harry J. Lemley.

The Board presented witnesses from the school staff to demonstrate that public sentiment had greatly changed, that there was organized disorder inside the school, that teachers were under an intolerable strain and that it was impossible to carry on a normal educational program with soldiers patrolling the halls. On June 21, Judge Lemley granted the Board's request for a period of delay on the understanding that the integration program would be resumed after two and one-half years. His ruling was immediately appealed by the NAACP on the grounds that it was "an invitation to violence."

The Eighth Circuit Court of Appeals at St. Louis heard the appeal on August 5. Attorney House told the Court that the School Board had not "voluntarily" surrendered to opposition to its plan. But, he said, "a school board cannot enforce integration. They . . . are there to help educate children. They should not have to get into unending, vicious turmoil with all their neighbors. You can't expect them to enforce integration."

Thurgood Marshall, general counsel for the NAACP, replied that the School Board had been lax in enforcing discipline at Central High School and said that if a cooling-off period was permitted it would be seized on by segregationists throughout the South to delay integration. "Democracy is a tough job," he added, "and integration in any community is not easy." He argued that if the Lemley decision stood, it would be a sign to segregationists that they could be successful anywhere "if they commit overt acts like arson or bombing."

On August 18, the appeals court set aside the Lemley order suspending integration in a six-to-one decision just sixteen days before the opening of school. The decision said that the issue was whether public resistance including mob violence constituted sufficient cause "to nullify an order of the federal court directing the Board to proceed with its integration plan. We say that the time has not yet come in these United States when an order of a federal court must be whittled away, watered down or shamefully withdrawn in the face of violent and unlawful acts of individual citizens. . . ." In a dissenting opinion, Chief Judge Archibald K. Gardner said that such changes as integration in Arkansas "if successful, are usually accomplished by evolution rather than revolution, and time, patience and forbearance are important elements in effecting all radical changes."

The appeals court granted the School Board a stay of execution to allow time for an appeal to the United States Supreme Court.

Senator John L. McClellan of Arkansas said in Washington that the decision was "rather tragic" and Senator J. William Fulbright said that "I deeply regret the court's decision. It presents the people of Arkansas with a very unhappy situation." Congressman Brooks Hays said that the decision "poses a difficult problem" for the community leadership. President Eisenhower issued a statement saying that his "feelings are exactly the same" as they were when he ordered federal troops to Little Rock and Governor Faubus replied that his attitude, too, was unchanged.

III

Governor Faubus had won the Democratic nomination, tantamount to election in Arkansas, for a third term by a landslide vote on July 29. His political prestige in the state as a whole had never been greater. As soon as the Lemley decision was reversed, he summoned a special session of the Legislature. The School Board, still caught in the middle, postponed the opening of school until its position could be clarified.

The state legislators gathered in Little Rock with the segregationists riding high, wide and handsome. The temper of the public generally was such that they knew there would be no serious opposition to legal measures designed to thwart integration. I was personally acquainted with a large percentage of the legislators and I talked to many of them. As I knew, not a few were moderate or liberal men and were distressed by what was happening. "I don't like it at all," a number of them told me. "But in this situation I am helpless. I would not mind for a moment losing my seat in the Legislature, but I can't afford to vote against Faubus because my business would suffer."

The special session met on August 26 for the announced purpose of regulating the administration and financing of public schools and education. Faubus proposed an anti-integration program that was incorporated in six bills—others were also offered by some legislators—and by nightfall they were well on their way toward enactment. Two days later the bills were approved with hardly a dissenting vote and sent to the Governor. The principal measures giving the Governor arbitrary power over schools, provided:

1. The Governor could close any or all schools when he alone determined that closing was necessary to preserve peace or when court-ordered integration was enforced by troops or marshals, or when he determined that a suitable educational system could not be maintained because of integration.

2. A local option election on a "yes" or "no" basis to decide on complete integration or no integration at all.

3. If a school was ordered closed, any member of a school board or any school official who failed to implement the order would be subject to immediate removal by the Governor, who could temporarily appoint his successor.

4. State funds of closed schools would be withheld on a per-pupil basis and paid to whatever other public school or accredited non-profit private school the pupils attended. State aid to schools would be withheld and transferred on the same basis.

5. Any student in an area where integration was imminent or in effect could transfer to a nonintegrated school and classes could be segregated within an integrated school.

6. Any person attempting to interfere with students' choices of classes or schools could be fined and sentenced to jail if convicted.

In addition, the Legislature passed bills providing for recall of school board members by a majority vote and aimed at curtailing activities of such organizations as the NAACP.

A mere recital of the legislation does not indicate the power that had accrued to the Governor—and, of course, to his political machine. The effect of segregationist influence, of the re-election of Faubus to a third term and of the acts slavishly passed by the legislators reached far beyond school affairs. Just for example, the very important State High Commission, which controlled huge contracts and decided where roads should be extended, had been wisely taken "out of politics" before Faubus became Governor. This was partly done by extending terms of the five commissioners to ten years and by staggering appointments so that no governor in the usual two terms would have a chance to appoint a majority of the Commission unless there was a death or resignation. Actually, a member of the Commission died during the summer of 1958 but it was near the end of Faubus' second term and the Governor avoided any criticism during the election campaign by appointing one of the authors of the bill that had removed the Commission from politics.

But when Faubus became the first governor in fifty years to be elected to a third term he was able to appoint a fourth commissioner and thus his appointees constituted a majority of the commission. "When his appointees . . . became a majority," the *Arkansas Gazette* said editorially, "their first official act was to force the resignation of Highway Director Herbert Eldridge— against whom no charge was ever brought except that he was independent of importuning politicians. . . . No one can misread that handwriting on the wall."

Perhaps it can be said that Faubus did not immediately use many of his legal extraordinary powers, which were, in fact, being challenged by test suits in the state courts. But the point was not what powers he exercised. The fact was that he had the powers. He was backed by an aggressive political machine led by men who sought influence for personal and business reasons. He was supported by an extremist minority that recklessly used the weapons of propaganda and boycott and economic reprisal. It did not matter whether this combination constituted, in fact, a regime that was powerful and ruthless. It was enough that it was feared. The result was the same.

Just as one example of the political climate, let me cite the case of a reporter for the *Arkansas Democrat* who wrote a humorous article poking fun at the Legislature. "Senator Jerry Screeton became irate," the Hot Springs *Sentinel-Record* reported. "The upper chamber, at Mr. Screeton's oratorical and gesturing behest, issued a 48-hour ultimatum to the *Democrat* demanding an apology, which it didn't get. It then banned all *Democrat* reporters except one . . . a favorite of the legislators and Governor Faubus. . . . Wrath was vented by removing the newspaper's name plate from [the reporter's] desk and replacing it with one bearing the reporter's name. . . . We suggest . . . retaining the services of a staff dermatologist to treat thin skins of some legislators suffering from overexposure to the press." In addition, the House denied the usual press accommodations on the floor to the *Arkansas Legislative Digest*, which had been critical of Faubus.

IV

While the Legislature was racing to pass the segregation bills before the Supreme Court acted on our cooling-off period plea, President Eisenhower acknowledged at a press conference in Washington that he might have told friends—as reported in *Newsweek* magazine—he was in favor of a slower approach to desegregation.

"It might have been that I said something about 'slower,'" he said, "but I do believe that we should—because I do say, as I did yesterday or last week, we have to have reason and sense and education, and a lot of other developments that go hand in hand as this process—if this process is going to have any real acceptance in the United States."

The NAACP was quick to react through its executive secretary, saying that "it seems incredible that the President with all of the channels of information available to him should have decided four and a half years [after the Supreme Court's integration decision] that the pace should be slower."

The Supreme Court didn't get around to deciding on the appeal by the School Board until September 12, but then it affirmed the decision of the Eighth Circuit Court of Appeals that no further delay in integration could be authorized.

I had been in Washington for the Supreme Court hearing and that evening I flew back to Little Rock. Attorney Butler and I were surrounded by a crowd of newspapermen as we got off the airplane.

"Did you know that one of the School Board—Mr. Rath—had resigned?" they asked. I didn't know it until then.

"Did you know the state police are looking for you?" another asked.

I didn't know that either and, as a matter of fact, they didn't find me that evening. The police mistakenly thought that I was driving into town with Butler and they followed his automobile. Meanwhile, I had met a friend who drove me home. But early the next morning, the police found me and served on me a proclamation by Governor Faubus closing all senior high schools in Little Rock on the basis of the segregation bills enacted by the Legislature. He also ordered a special election to be held late in September when the people could vote only "yes" or "no" on complete integration or no integration at all. This proposition obviously was not designed to give a true test of community sentiment and it was carried by the anti-integrationists with 70 per cent of the ballots cast.

All three senior high schools, with 3,700 students, were shut down but the School Board sought to prevent complete disbandment of the staff by continuing to pay teachers for the school year, about $720,000 in all, while the validity of the state segregation laws was being tested in the courts. When the Board canceled the football schedule, there was a storm of protest—Little Rock had three top-notch football teams—and Faubus joined the outcry by charging that the closure was inhuman. As a result, the Board said it would carry out the football schedule and anything else that the Governor would return to it. Only football was returned, and football was all we offered the youth of Little Rock that year.

An attempt was made to organize private schools and lease the public school facilities. The Board agreed to this plan in order to facilitate a court test of its legality. On September 17, the Little Rock Private School Corporation was granted a charter by the Pulaski County circuit court and Faubus announced in a television speech the plans for a segregated school, based on a state constitutional provision adopted in 1874. He contended that state funds could be used to aid the school and that public school facilities could be leased. But the NAACP, supported by the Department of Justice, quickly secured a federal court injunction against leasing of public school facilities, and the plan collapsed when the School Board and teachers refused to defy the court order.

"The burden of making a determination [of whether to have integrated public schools or none at all] shifts now to the community leadership—public and private—which has remained largely silent through the last troubled year," the *Arkansas Gazette* said editorially. "The simple running of time will not in itself bring any answers. If we are to avoid sacrificing a year's education for most of our high school students, and the prospect of grave permanent damage to our public school system, the people of Little Rock are going to have to find an alternative on their own motion—and they are going to have to find it soon."

This was doubtless good advice, but no effective leadership appeared. The senior high schools remained closed. On October 20, the Little Rock Private School Corporation opened a private high school in the former University of Arkansas Graduate Center, and announced that donations, which were its sole source of income, totaled $61,481.25. The private school corporation attempted to hire teachers from the public school system, but none of them would take jobs. Later, Dr. T. J. Raney, who was president of the corporation, asked me to become its superintendent, presumably in the belief that such a move would persuade some of the public school teachers to sign contracts. I refused.

The private school eventually had around 800 students. A newspaper survey showed that some 2,200 of the city's 3,700 high school students had enrolled in private schools of one kind or another or had transferred to public schools elsewhere, or were taking correspondence courses. The other 1,500 were presumed to be without any schooling. This situation tended to give the city a different appearance. Even casual visitors, familiar with Little Rock in the past, sometimes called my attention to the absence of the usual number of children on the streets in the evening, particularly on a Friday night. Many children, of course, had left the city to attend schools elsewhere but it was also true that parents were more inclined to restrict the evening activities of their children because of racial tension in the community.

V

The wrecking of the school system was by no means the only damage to the community of Little Rock. The city had been in the midst of a period of rapid growth, of industrial boom. In 1955, the Chamber of Commerce published a list of nineteen new industries in the community. In the next couple of years, up through the summer of 1957, fifteen other companies bought from 2 to 168 acres and built new plants. A new 600-acre industrial district was established on the edge of the city. Then the school integration crisis began. In the next eighteen months, up to the time this is written, not a single new company decided to move into the industrial area, although three that had previously made arrangements came in the fall of 1957.

In January of 1959, the Little Rock branch of the American Association of University Women released a survey in which they asked eighty-five businessmen if the school situation had affected their business. Forty-four replied that their business had been hurt. In this group were seven of the eight real estate agents surveyed, five of the six drug store owners or managers, three of the four variety store managers and five of the six independent store owners. Six reported improved business but two of these were moving companies, one was a cleaning plant and three were service stations. It may be significant that during the height of the crisis one moving company official said in a letter to the newspapers that the city was being severely damaged by the loss of families who were moving elsewhere.

An article in the *Arkansas Recorder*, a digest of state government news, but with no official connections, said that in 1958 bonds issued by local industrial development organizations to attract new industry to all parts of Arkansas dropped to less than half of the total which were sold in 1957. "From January 1, 1958, to date [December, 1958] only $711,500 of local industrial development corporation bonds have been issued and of the 1957 $2,050,000 total, all but $120,000 were issued prior to September, 1957, when the Little Rock integration controversy first made headlines around the world," the article said. "The figures . . . were taken from a compilation by State Board of Finance Secretary Frank Storey of all local industrial development corporation bond issues in which the state has invested its funds. . . ."

There was a general effort by state officials to ignore the damage to business, but in the winter of 1959 the manager of the Little Rock Chamber of Commerce made the facts clear in a speech. He said that any large company planning to build a branch plant in Little Rock had to consider whether conditions there would be suitable for its key personnel and their families, including children of high school age. He then asked members of the Chamber to decide for themselves whether conditions were such that they would want to move their families to Little Rock.

The closure of the high schools, even if only for a year, could not fail to impair the long-term effectiveness of the city's staff of teachers. Those who had no pupils, although they continued to be paid, soon became restless and worried. This restlessness spread to teachers in other schools that were still open and many of them came to me with anxious questions about the future.

How long could things go on this way? they asked me repeatedly. Could the school system recover if the crisis were ended? What was going to happen to children suddenly shut out of classrooms and forced to suffer the brunt of a controversy for which they had no responsibility? Why did the people of the state stand by and see their system of public education threatened with destruction?

"I have always been very proud of the educational system we have built up here," one veteran woman teacher said. "But the Legislature doesn't seem to care what happens to it. The people don't seem to care. And, frankly, I'm not proud any longer. Even at best, it would take years to repair the damage."

Many of the teachers in all of the schools were naturally worried about the future and about the danger of losing their retirement pay. Not a few school boards in other cities tried to hire some of them away. In this period, I discovered that my biggest job was to try to keep up staff morale, to encourage the teachers to wait it out so that the city's children would not suffer the further catastrophe of one day returning to schools which had lost the most experienced and able teachers. I did my best to keep the staff intact and, while I was there, only one teacher resigned.

Perhaps the greatest damage of the integration crisis at Little Rock was in the field of human values. The formerly good relations between the races collapsed during a year of controversy and were replaced by bitterness and suspicion. In the past, the problems of the community, including integration, had been discussed openly and in a co-operative way by whites and Negroes alike, but in 1958 this ability to communicate with each other had virtually disappeared. There was a split within the Negro community as well, because many of the younger people had become resentful and impatient with delay and frustration, while the older Negroes were more inclined to accept their fate.

The white community was no better off. There were numerous resignations of lay people from positions of responsibility in the churches because they objected to the liberal attitude of certain ministers toward integration. One group of Methodists met in Little Rock in an unsuccessful attempt to form a splinter church organization. The subject of integration became so distasteful that even in church you could often hear sighs of despair if it was mentioned by the minister. There were so many hot-tempered arguments, so many splits in families or between partners that most people came to a point where they refused even to discuss integration. They could keep the peace only by keeping silent. Thus, not only was communication between the races extinguished, but the hope of some agreement among the white population died away. Only the extremists continued to speak out and they spoke for extreme solutions. The cause of moderation, of compromise, of progress flickered dimly because the moderate was the man who had been caught in the middle and had taken a terrible beating from both sides. He had been buffeted by the federal courts when he sought relief from an intolerable situation, and he had been boycotted by the segregationists when he suggested that a reasonable plan to move forward toward compromise might be preferable to a hysterical process of moving backward.

The extremists tried almost everything in the course of the controversy but the boycott obviously was their most effective weapon. They used it against various individuals or against firms that employed individuals to whom they objected. One large company serving several Southern states was severely damaged because one of its employees was a member of the School Board who stood, not for integration, but for observance of the law. The *Arkansas Gazette*, which won two 1958 Pulitzer Prize awards for its steadfast support of law observance, its civic leadership and its "dispassionate" editorials, was bitterly attacked by Faubus and boycotted by segregationists, who temporarily reduced its circulation sufficiently to cause an estimated loss of $250,000 in advertising revenue.

The viciousness of the campaign against the *Gazette* was illustrated by a letter sent to the advertising departments of many business firms and, incidentally, reproduced on the front page of the newspaper, which described it as a "deliberate distortion" of the paper's editorial policy. The letter said that a "massive crusade" was planned against stores in Little Rock that advertised in the *Gazette* because the newspaper had "played a leading role in breaking down our segregation laws." This was completely untrue, because the newspaper had supported every legal effort to maintain the social patterns of segregation and had only protested against "naked defiance of the law."

The boycott letter said that the "crusade" against the *Gazette* would be extended to a boycott of any store that advertised in the newspaper and last until such advertising ceased. "There is a rising tide of race feeling—in fact a revolution is beginning in the South and Little Rock," the letter concluded. "Your store and all stores that advertise in the *Arkansas Gazette* will be placed on one side or the other. This is your notice to make your own choice."

Propaganda against the *Gazette* was widely distributed. The people were urged to harass the newspaper by telephone or by putting envelope stickers on their mail saying: "I do not trade with those who advertise in the Gazette." Cards were circulated listing the telephone numbers of the *Gazette* and its executive editor. For weeks, segregationists made a practice of ringing the newspaper on pay telephones, leaving the receiver off the hook and walking away, thus tying up the newspaper's lines in an effort to interfere with its business office and its editorial staff.

But the effect of such boycotts was far greater than temporary damage to a few companies. The threat of boycott reached almost everywhere in fearsome fashion and caused countless men and women to remain silent or to knuckle under to the extremist minority. Time after time I heard men say that they were in complete sympathy with the School Board, but they added: "Don't use my name because I can't afford it."

After the senior high schools had been closed by Faubus in the fall of 1958, five members of the School Board—Dr. Dale Alford not included—decided that things would have to get worse before there was any hope of improvement. To illustrate this viewpoint to the public, the five decided to resign en masse.

"We've been the whipping boy for the Governor all through this," one member explained. "We tried to obey the law and to find a reasonable solution to the problem. Now let's force Faubus to get a new whipping boy and that will show the people that this crisis is not just due to a blundering School Board but that integration must be faced no matter who is on the Board.

When this decision became known, several prominent citizens decided to call a private meeting of the city's business and civic leaders in an effort to plan some kind of solution. About thirty-five men, all in the top rank of business, attended and their first action was to urge the five School Board members to reconsider. They declined.

Then the meeting considered a proposal that can be summed up this way: "The threat of boycott has paralyzed every effort to provide constructive leadership. There are six positions on the School Board. It just happens that there are six banks in Little Rock. The presidents or chairmen of the boards of these banks are all prominent citizens, and if all six would run for the School Board they would almost certainly be elected. Thus every bank in the city would be in the same position and it would be impossible for the segregationists to boycott any one bank. Therefore, the School Board will be free to present a reasonable program to solve the crisis."

This seemed an ingenious idea to everybody except the bankers.

"Our banks would not be protected at all," one of them told the meeting. "For example, we depend heavily on the subsidiary deposits of banks in eastern Arkansas, where segregationist sentiment is strongest. If they withdrew their deposits and transferred them to banks in Memphis—as they doubtless would—we would immediately be in trouble."

The bankers agreed to consider the proposal. Some of them

wanted to try it but the attitude of the meeting generally was deeply pessimistic. It was at this meeting that one prominent businessman declared that "you had all just as well recognize we are living in a police state."

"I never before understood," commented another, "how it was that Hitler and Mussolini were able to exercise dictatorial power over so many people. Now I know from experience how they took over."

Later the bankers, as a group, rejected the proposal to seek election to the School Board, and at the next election a strongly segregationist Board was chosen. I do not wish to point a finger at the bankers, however. Almost everybody else was in the same boat. Perhaps fifty prominent citizens refused requests that they seek election to the School Board. And, so far as I know, not a single educator in Arkansas endangered his institution's standing with the Legislature or risked loss of his job by speaking up boldly against a situation that, in the long run, could only destroy the state's system of free public education.

Chapter Fifteen

IT NEED NOT
HAPPEN AGAIN

THIS IS ABOUT the end of my story of the Little Rock school crisis, because just before a solidly segregationist School Board took office in December of 1958, my supporters on the retiring Board terminated my contract without cause and without prejudice. I suppose that the attitude of at least part of the community had changed in regard to me as well as in regard to gradual integration. In any event, I had come a far piece from the day in 1955 when I was selected Man of the Year for Little Rock.

In connection with the School Board's action, I would like to cite one minor example of what could happen in the political climate that had been established in Little Rock. The Board authorized that I should be paid for the remainder of my contract after my services ended on November 30, 1958. This was not approved by those who had opposed integration. A suit was filed to prevent the payment and Chancery Judge Murray Reed issued an order temporarily restraining the treasurer of the school district from turning the money over to me. The next day the treasurer called me.

"I've got a problem," he said. "As I read the restraining order, I can't even pay you your salary for the month of November. Maybe you should get Judge Reed to issue an order for me to pay you that much."

I called Judge Reed and asked if it was intended by the court that I should be deprived of my salary for November.

"I don't know," he answered. "I didn't read the order. I just signed it. I guess you better ask the lawyer who filed the suit."

There wasn't much else I could do. I called the lawyer, James Sloan, and he said he would telephone the Judge and tell him that my November salary was not included in the temporary restraining order. I guess he did, because I later got my pay for November. But that didn't do anything to relieve my depression over what the state of Arkansas had come to when the meaning of a court order was decided, temporarily at least, not by a duly elected judge, but by the lawyer who had filed suit against me.

I was in agreement with the School Board when it terminated my contract, but I wasn't happy about it because I don't give up easily. I firmly believe that our phase plan of gradual integration was the best that could have been formulated for Little Rock and I deeply regretted not being permitted to see it through to the end. Even ardent segregationists had originally told me it was the best they could hope for in the long run and the NAACP was willing to accept it because they had discovered they were not likely to get court authority for speedier integration. It was, in fact, specifically tailored for our school district, as any successful integration in the South must be fitted to local conditions.

Why, then, did our plan fail?

Looking back, I suppose any objective observer would see that we faced many unexpected developments, that we had to improvise at times and that we made mistakes. But I believe the basic reasons for failure must be found in the vacillation of political leaders at state and federal levels—all tried to avoid responsibility for enforcement—and in a deliberate plot by segregationists all over the South to force a finish fight in Little Rock in an effort to delay or prevent a showdown on their own home grounds.

In the first place, the Supreme Court's order for school integration with "all deliberate speed" seemed to recognize that compliance would take longer in some areas than in others. Some states, such as Missouri, immediately changed state segregation laws to comply with the Court decisions. In other states, such as Kentucky and Tennessee, there were state and local officials who co-operated in programs for integration. But still other states, such as Virginia and Georgia, did the exact opposite by refusing to plan for integration and passing laws designed to nullify the Supreme Court decisions. This "all deliberate speed" gave the segregationists an opportunity to make a test fight in Little Rock and to use the argument that the people did not have to accept integration because other areas in the South had no integration plan. It was an effective argument as far as the public was concerned.

"We won't comply with the Supreme Court decisions," a Mississippi orator summed up for a Little Rock audience. "We will resist as long as we can. Then we will defy the Court and secede from the Union. And then—we will apply to Washington for foreign aid."

Even so, politics was the most important factor in our defeat. The Supreme Court decisions put politicians at all levels on "the hot seat" and most of them were busier trying to get off the seat than they were trying to enforce the law. The fate of a few state officials who sought to observe the law or to find a compromise solution was enough to convince many others that moderation meant political suicide. Governor Frank Clement of Tennessee, who stood firm against the segregationist threats, did not even run for re-election. Congressman Brooks Hays of Little Rock, who attempted to find a reasonable compromise solution, was defeated in 1958 by Dale Alford, the School Board's outspoken segregationist. Oddly enough Alford had voted for the original motion in 1955 for adoption by the School Board of our gradual integration plan—not because he favored integration but presumably because the Board's attorneys had said it represented a legal minimum of integration.

By 1958, moderation had become a liability and cleverness at evading or delaying compliance with the law became the key to political survival. "You have to be an extremist to survive in Arkansas," a veteran politician remarked to me. "You have to out-faubus Faubus to get the votes."

This game of evading responsibility did not stop at state boundaries. The Department of Justice presented no plan for supporting local attempts to carry out integration, and a federal judge refused to supply U.S. marshals to protect Central High School at a time when, I am confident, any show of action by the federal government would have been more than welcome to Faubus. "What are the federals going to do?" the Governor asked me repeatedly before he threw himself into the arms of the segregationists. I could only assume that he hoped the "federals" would take vigorous enforcement action, thus rescuing him from the political "hot seat" and permitting him to evade responsibility for enforcement or nonenforcement.

Even after mob action had forced the President to send federal troops to Little Rock, the Department of Justice did not release the FBI report on responsibility for the disorders, nor did it take action against known rioters. One day when I was in the office of U.S. Attorney Cobb, an FBI agent handed him a packet of papers.

"These are completed cases against four persons involved in the disorders," Cobb told me. "We will move for indictments against them."

But he didn't. I later asked him about the indictments but I never found out why the cases were dropped. Not a single person was indicted, although even in Little Rock municipal court one person was fined and six others were given suspended fines as a result of the school disorders. How could respect for the law prevail if those who flouted it went unpunished?

Attorney General Brownell resigned on October 23, 1957, and some dispatches from Washington said that the "settling" of federal policy in the Little Rock crisis—whatever that meant—had freed him to return to private law practice. He was succeeded by William P. Rogers. On November 21, the *Arkansas Gazette* said that dispatches from Washington and information at Cobb's office made it clear the federal government would not prosecute suspected agitators unless further trouble developed. In December, when segregationists were working vigorously to close Central High School, dispatches quoted Rogers as saying "we ought to give the Little Rock matter a chance to rest awhile." A year later, just before Faubus closed the high schools, Rogers said in a Los Angeles speech that the state governments had an "affirmative responsibility" to maintain order so that the rights of individuals, as determined by the courts, would be protected and that "no further occasion need arise—none should be permitted to arise—which would require the federal government to act. . . ."

Finally, the Little Rock integration program suffered severely from lack of positive leadership in the city government. Mayor Mann spoke out for law and order, but we were in the middle of a change to a city manager administration, and Mann was a lame-duck mayor without real political power or prestige. He feuded with the City Council and with the Governor and political bickering further weakened local leadership.

All of these things combined to contribute to the success—however temporary—of the segregationists. Even the fact that most of the people of Little Rock originally were ready to accept our integration plan worked against us in the end, because we did not expect trouble and were surprised and unprepared when, as I have related, trouble was thrust upon us by outsiders.

II

Where do we go from here?

I can speak only as a school administrator who believes the dignity of the individual is a fundamental part of our American heritage. First, we must face existing facts. The Supreme Court's school integration decisions are here to stay, as demonstrated by its decisions in the Little Rock case. At the same time, the Court's approval of the Alabama pupil placement law, permitting the School Board to transfer students for reasons other than race, means that a high degree of segregation can sometimes be maintained to preserve educational standards. Thus, the way is open to accept the inevitable in a lawful manner with intelligence instead of emotion. And one thing is obvious—if the South does not plan the future of its system of public education in line with the mainstream of progress, then the federal government will step in and do it for us.

To make the most of our opportunity to progress, any existing vacuums in leadership at national and state levels must be filled. There must be leadership to convince the people that compliance is essential to their own welfare as well as to our national security in a troubled world. It must be leadership for vigorous enforcement of integration programs fitted to local conditions and carried out through civil—not military—processes.

The present federal Civil Rights Commission should be continued to study, analyze and recommend strengthened legislation to aid minorities. I believe, too, that we need a national community relations commission which would foster strong local leadership in favor of preservation of free public education and in favor of respect for the law. Such a commission would not be concerned with moral or sociological arguments but, by taking a positive approach and drawing on experience in such cities as Little Rock, it could help local leaders prepare in advance to prevent integration crises. There is, in addition, far more to school desegregation than mere compliance. Many important technical problems arise, involving the lag in educational standards in Negro schools and the meshing of pupil records or the curricula of widely different schools. I believe the Department of Health, Education and Welfare should stand ready to provide guidance of an expert nature, if requested by a school board or a federal court, in order to solve such problems with the least possible confusion and the least possible waste of tax money.

I do not believe that any private school system can be organized to meet the needs of all the children of the South. Public education has long been the great strength of America. We now face an era, both at home and in world affairs, when we must have the best possible educational system. I believe any weakening of free public education endangers our nation's future. But to avoid that danger, there must be leadership that will open the countless minds now closed to any argument even for token integration. This leadership must face the difficult task of separating civil rights from social rights—that is, make clear that school integration has no relation to the social problem of interracial marriage.

This problem is of great and sincere concern to the South, and social affairs will certainly be drastically curtailed or eliminated in integrated schools. I can only say, in this connection, that no community can afford to be without public education and that many present schools would be better off with less emphasis on social affairs and more emphasis on education.

It has been suggested that this problem also might be met by segregation of the sexes within integrated schools, but I cannot agree. In the first place, I believe proper training in the home and in the churches will obviate most social problems. But, beyond that, the purpose of education is not to protect children from the problems of life. It is to train them so they will know how to handle the situations they must face if they are to live full and successful lives. Segregation by sexes could be only a deterrent to the development of white pupils.

To assure successful integration of Southern schools, I believe there should be stronger federal civil rights legislation designed to crack down hard against bombing or destruction of school property, against scurrilous propaganda attacks on the courts and on school authorities and against abuse of the right of peaceable assembly near school grounds. The Department of Justice should be given power to initiate injunctive proceedings against those who interfere with law enforcement instead of leaving it to school officials to assume the untenable position of seeking court restraint of their neighbors. Illegal acts must be punished if the law is to be respected, but moderate and able citizens will refuse to assume civic leadership if they, rather than duly chosen public officials, must act to enforce the law. Many prominent persons did refuse to serve on the Little Rock School Board for that reason, and the segregationists took control.

But most important of all, perhaps, the people of the South must come to realize that, with desegregation the law of the land, every school district will be better off if it complies intelligently by planning its own program instead of delaying until the federal government steps in to enforce school integration. There cannot be any single, standardized program for all. Each community is different and each plan should be unique. Some may find it best to start integration in the primary grades as was done at Nashville. Others may prefer to start at college levels and work down through secondary and elementary grades, as was done in St. Louis. Or complete immediate integration—as at Louisville—may be the best solution. However it may be done, I am confident that local planning in line with local conditions will be essential to preserve standards of education, to protect the rights of the community and the state and to maintain the dignity of Americans.

I do not want to leave any impression that school integration in the South will be easy or rapid. Far from it. Progress is seldom easy; the transformation of a traditional way of life in which millions of persons sincerely believe is impossible without pain and anguish. There will be resistance, sometimes bitter resistance. In some areas today the people will not consider any kind of integration. They won't even talk about compliance with the law. But the law is still there, and it won't disappear no matter how tightly they close their eyes or their minds.

Little Rock was a classic example of what a community should not let extremists do to it. I did not believe it could happen. It did happen, despite the untiring efforts of members of the School Board, members of the school staff and many others with whom I am proud to have been associated. It can happen again, somewhere, some way.

But I don't believe it will happen again in the same way. It is no longer possible to escape the realization that the future of our system of public education is at stake, that the future of thousands upon thousands of wonderful young people depends on respect for the law. I hold a fundamental conviction that the South will intelligently and ably face, not to the illusory past, but to the high promise of our nation's future.

Index